TIMMY'S RESCUE

− One Lil' Waif at a Time −

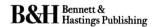

B&H Bennett &
Hastings Publishing

TESTIMONIALS

A touching and inspiring testament to how big a heart can grow. Rebecca, Evangelynn, and the rest of the Lil' Waif support crew are amazing examples of dedication and compassion, not only enriching the lives of hundreds of pups, but also all the lucky owners who were matched with each one. As owners of one of the Lil' Waif pups (Sienna's crew), we have been blessed with a very special canine companion who fills our own hearts every day. We are truly grateful to Lil' Waif for their service and mission to this important cause.

-Jason and Joyce Frazier
(Puppy Parents)

Timmy's Rescue is a well written and heartfelt account of the trials and joyful moments involved with operating a dog rescue organization. It is inspirational and walks the reader through the journey of so many sweet dogs who are a testament to the amazing canine spirit. It brought me to tears, made me laugh and I know after reading this book I will have an even more tender place in my heart for the rescue dogs and organizations with whom I work as a veterinarian.

- Dr. Marguerite Gleason
The Carolinas Animal Hospital and Dental Clinic
Charlotte, NC
(Veterinarian)

Timmy's Rescue, One Lil' Waif At A Time , is a poignant book about the strength and selflessness of Rebecca Kizanis, her family and many brave rescue workers as they navigate their way through creating a puppy rescue in western Washington. Each riveting account in the book tells a story of their courage and sacrifice in the name of saving the lives of helpless, abused and severely neglected dogs and puppies. In this eye-opening narrative, you are taken inside many rescue attempts, some quite dangerous, and your heart pounds with hope and anticipation that the rescuers will be safe and the dogs will be saved. Lil' Waif Puppy Rescue remembers all of the dogs that others have forgotten.

After reading this book, you will be inspired to do more and to make a difference, just as Lil' Waif has.

-Florence Bernhard, Animal Behaviorist
The Tail Wagger's Club
(Animal Behaviorist)

It's been our great privilege to work with Rebecca and Evangelynn of Lil' Waif Puppy Rescue. First meeting as acquaintances working together to save homeless pets, our relationship has grown to one of deep respect and friendship. Lil' Waif Rescue's doors are always open whenever we call for their help. It never matters if the puppies are large or small, purebred or mutt, if there's just one or a litter of twelve, they are always welcomed with Rebecca's and Evangelynn's loving and knowledgeable open arms. Lil' Waif Puppy Rescue's grace, honesty and dedication make it a shining star of hope for homeless puppies. For the rest of us in pet rescue, it's a star we'd all do well in following.

-Marian Moore & Mike Flory
Founders Yakima Valley Pet Rescue
(YVPR Founders)

Rebecca and Evangelynn described our pups and their personalities exactly. They helped us choose the perfect pups for our lifestyle. Fred has always been spirited and funny. He is quite the gymnast, performing somersaults when excited. Ruby is snoopy and adorable. Her oversized ears never miss a word (or a crumb). Thanks to Lil' Waif, our uniquely wonderful canine companions enrich our lives so much, we don't even care if they cause mayhem in the garden every now and then.

-Ciscoe and Mary Morris
(Puppy Parents)

PUPPIES AT PLAY

TIMMY'S RESCUE

– One Lil' Waif at a Time –

from overcrowded, noisy shelters to a puppy haven called
Lil' Waif

Lil' Waif Puppy Rescue
REBECCA R. KIZANIS

To Timmy

May you know what you inspired.

Author's Note

The events narrated in this book are based largely on the author's recollection of real events that she and her family members experienced. To protect privacy and avoid possible legal ramifications, the names of some individuals have been changed and identifiable details modified.

In March 2002, the doors of an ordinary, suburban-family household opened to welcome orphaned puppies into what would become an in-home rescue and safe haven named Lil' Waif Puppy Rescue. What started seven years ago as a mission to save puppies, and the occasional adult dog, continues in hopes that the dream of having no more unwanted companions will one day become reality.

This is the story of Lil' Waif Puppy Rescue and their journey into the mission of rescue.

CONTENTS

CONTENTS

Adopting Timmy

Baby Timmy

Ah, Timmy …. We found each other at a small rescue organization where my daughter and I volunteered. Pulling that furry little bundle out of the crate made my heart race, and once he was in my arms, our hearts instantly intertwined. I had not intended to adopt a puppy, but Timmy, I knew, was meant to be mine.

This sweet little puppy's leg dangled from his small body. Veterinarians seemed to agree that the puppy's leg had been broken at a very young age, possibly when he was just a week old. Since we found him when the Christmas season was approaching and he was a little tyke hobbling about, we named him Timmy (after Charles Dickens' inspiring character in *A Christmas Carol*) and affectionately called him, "Tiny Tim," a nickname we kept, even as he grew into a 90-lb dog.

Although the success of surgery was questionable, we decided to go ahead with it, in hopes of restoring Timmy's mobility. We had the procedure performed by an orthopedic specialist, and I was able to bring this sweet puppy home the day before Thanksgiving. That holiday season, our family's Thanksgiving and Christmas centered on Timmy, my new little puppy with the big red cast. As he lay in his bed on the couch, someone was always next to him rubbing those long, soft ears.

Timmy was recovering from surgery during a time that is highly important to a puppy's social development. I was determined that he would not miss out on social experiences during that small window of opportunity. We took field trips: to the elementary school to meet children, to grocery stores where we sat outside so customers could pet him, to pet stores to meet other dogs, and to movie theaters where people of all sorts would stop to meet the sweet little puppy with a cast. Sometimes Timmy was carried in a child carrier; sometimes he was pulled in a wagon or pushed in a stroller. I was thrilled at how he seemed to love the attention of children and other dogs.

I had it all planned out in my mind: once Timmy's leg was healed we were going to start obedience classes. I felt certain Timmy would be the star; after all, he was already my star. Then we would undertake therapy dog certification: once he passed his therapy dog evaluation, we would work together in hospitals and retirement centers. Timmy would make children happy in hospitals and the elderly would anxiously await our visits, to reminisce about their own past companions.

I was enjoying each day with Timmy, but his love made me even more aware of the fate of so many unwanted puppies and dogs. Was it fair that my baby boy Tim was getting so much love and attention while other dogs and puppies endured lives of hunger and loneliness? Some were cooped up in overcrowded, smelly shelters until it was their turn to take their last walk to "the back room."

The rescue center I had volunteered at and eventually adopted Tim from, was a first-class rescue operation. I thought, "Maybe they would be willing to take in dogs from other communities, from shelters that are overcrowded and where the dogs have no hope of being adopted." At the time, they were more focused on helping owner-surrendered dogs in the local community, but surprisingly, they agreed to accept a few dogs and puppies. We were excited: we had a start!

Amidst the excitement of contacting shelters and making plans for rescuing dogs, I thought that maybe I could bring a few into my home and list them on Petfinder®, an online national pet adoption resource. I had a large, finished basement that had been well-used as my five daughters were growing up but now stood empty. I had always wanted to have puppies, but bringing a litter into the world seemed irresponsible when millions of dogs are put down each year because they don't have homes. Maybe this would be my opportunity to have a litter of puppies ... Oh, little did I know what the years ahead would bring!

BEGINNINGS

One of my adult daughters, Trulie, had been working in dog rescue, specializing in Pointers. When Trulie told us about an eastern Washington shelter that had puppies housed in poor conditions, we knew the moment had arrived to set up our first rescue.

Trulie made arrangements with the shelter. Despite the shelter's desperate need, they were wary of having people come in to take dogs; they were concerned about our motives and about the shelter receiving poor publicity. One of the things they insisted on was that we keep the shelter's name confidential. We agreed. Even so, the shelter manager commented that it was just easier to adopt them to Jesus; implying he would rather euthanize a dog than go through the hassle of trying to get them into rescue. It was clear there was no guarantee that we would be able to take puppies home with us, but we prepared for the best. The night before our appointment, we arranged crates in two cars and stocked up with towels, water and anything else we thought we might need.

The next morning, Trulie and another of my adult daughters, Evangelynn, set out with me for the seven-hour drive from our home in the suburbs of Seattle. It was a new day in our lives, and we were full of hope for our work. Upon arrival at our destination, we stumbled out of the car, excited to pick out our puppies. Evangelynn and I were not prepared to deal with what we saw. We were directed to the "puppy room," where we found three or four litters all in concrete pens, soaking wet, cold and shivering. When we asked why they were all wet, they said they had just hosed down the pens. Although shocked, we nodded, smiled and said "oh," like it was the most normal thing to hose down a pen full of six- to eight-week old puppies. So there we stood, looking at so many round, hopeless eyes and wondering how we thought we could really choose from among them. How could we possibly look at their conditions and say, "We'll take this one, but not this one"?

I announced that we weren't leaving any of them; we were going to take them all. The girls nodded their agreement, in relief. Evangelynn and I started to rearrange the crates to accommodate so many little ones while Trulie negotiated with the shelter director in the little meeting room. I watched her through the window from the hall, smiling and laughing with him. I prayed that he would let us have the puppies. When she came out, she said tersely, "Okay, I struck a deal ... two for the price of one. Let's pay and get out of here."

We had told the Seattle rescue that we would bring back a couple nice adult dogs as well. After the process of settling the puppies into our cars was complete, we returned with heavy hearts to the shelter's hopeless halls. I knew we would see row after row of unloved dogs, and that those we did not pick would die a cold death by the following week. The number of dogs was overwhelming and equally heartbreaking; two or three to a kennel, some barking and demanding attention, others huddled in a corner, scared and alone. We were feeling rushed: the puppies were getting hot in the cars, Trulie was feeling very antsy, and lingering wasn't going to improve anything. We chose a couple of adult dogs, said thank you and left. At last, we were settled on a total of twenty-one puppies and two older dogs.

It took some work to get everyone loaded. We rearranged the crates, and then rearranged them again. Finally the cars were loaded, and we were all set to leave ... but I wanted to use the bathroom one last time. The girls rolled their eyes and instructed me to hurry, which I did. But on the way out, I decided to take just one more quick glance in the kennel holding the majority of adult dogs. Again, my heart broke as I looked at all the dogs. One dog in particular stood out, an eighty-pound female yellow Labrador Retriever. I am a sucker for Labs. I could not leave without her. The fact that both of the cars were full to capacity did not seem to register with me. I only knew that Molly (right then I named her Molly) was coming home with us.

Trulie and Evangelynn were pacing, wondering what was taking me so long. Their jaws dropped when they saw me exit the shelter with Molly. They shook their heads: there was no more room, no possible room, not even for a little puppy, and certainly not for a big Lab. But I had made up my mind, so it was decided that Molly would sit on my lap in the front passenger seat, for the duration of the seven-hour trip home. Well, Molly had no problem with that! She jumped right in, scooted her big self into a comfortable position, and thoroughly enjoyed her view of the scenery, smiling with her tail a-wagging. As for me, I could not move, see or even breathe at times … but I had rescued Molly, the big yellow Labrador. If I were to die right there from being smothered or crushed, I would die one happy rescuer.

Rescue work can feel like riding a roller coaster built on the tracks of your emotions. We were at an emotional high point that afternoon, driving home with our two carloads of puppies and dogs, but it quickly became apparent one litter of puppies was ill. They had severe diarrhea and vomiting, and appeared to be in pain. We spent many days at the vets and many days and nights nursing them, but we lost two of our four precious puppies.

That was our first experience with parvovirus (parvo), a horrendous and painful intestinal disease. In the earliest years, before we learned how to properly vaccinate and quarantine litters coming into our rescue, this disease would invade our new little rescue again and again, causing heartbreak and creating huge financial burdens. Canine rescue work has many rewards, but it is not without its sorrows.

"Flower," forever in our hearts, lost the battle to this deadly virus and passed over the Rainbow Bridge, 2002

ALL PAWS FORWARD

Our bleak beginning did not dampen our resolve. Losing those dear puppies inspired a greater determination to get orphaned puppies out of overcrowded shelters and into healthy homes. A couple of weeks after losing Flower, we were busy making plans for another trip to the shelter. We wanted to spare as many dogs as possible from a cold death in the back room.

This time we did more preliminary work. We contacted other local rescues, describing the shelter's conditions. To our delight, several rescues agreed to take a dog or puppies; one offering to take as many as three small, adult dogs. We sought advice from established rescues. One couple who ran a rescue drove out and helped us build a couple pens for the puppies. My husband, Dan, has built many more over the years, using the same basic design. We found out where to purchase vaccinations and how to administer them. We learned about quarantining puppies, and about best practices in nursing sick puppies.

I did not feel like I could take a step inside that shelter again, so when the girls suggested I stay home, I agreed. I helped load the Subaru with the crates and stood waving long after they were gone, praying for their safety. I knew they would make wise choices, not emotional ones, and bring home fewer puppies and dogs this time. And I was certain that they would not make the seven-hour drive home with a ninety-pound Labrador sitting on their lap!

About sixteen hours later, the girls pulled into our driveway, the little Subaru now filled with four-legged little waifs. They were met by myself and volunteers from other rescue groups, all of us excited to meet our prospective charges. Quickly, we began unloading dogs and puppies …. The more we unloaded, the more there seemed to be inside: it was like a clown car act! Finally I asked the girls, "Okay! How many are there?" There was a total of twenty-seven puppies and dogs. So much for me being the emotional one, unable to say "no"!

The girls told me that when they were paying and gathering the paperwork, a man came into the shelter leading a young, beautiful Aussie mix. He handed over the leash, said, "We're moving to an apartment that doesn't take dogs," then turned and walked out. The girls were horrified that someone could callously commit their dog to a loud, crowded concrete cell, knowing she would most likely spend a miserable week before being put down. The manager turned her attention to the girls, shrugged and said, "Do you want her? You can just take her. It would save me the paperwork." Despite the fact the car was already packed to capacity – and they were way over the promised quota – they didn't hesitate. So … as it turned out, I was not the only one at our rescue to learn what it feels like to sit seven hours with a big dog on your lap!

That day, many of the rescue groups took more dogs than they had originally planned, and we made room for the rest in our new puppy area. We were new to rescue and correspondingly naïve; we didn't fully understand the commitment rescue groups make for each dog. Volunteer dog rescuers are responsible for many tasks: finding foster homes, making sure that each dog is spayed or neutered, and caring for the dog's health until its adoption into an approved home. The last item alone can be very expensive and is almost always a rescue organization's main financial drain. Rescuers often have to train a dog to be housebroken and have basic manners, and sometimes they have to help a dog overcome major behavioral issues, like those associated with separation anxiety. These all need to be handled before a dog is deemed "adoptable." Then there are hours of screening and meeting with applicants and potential adopters. We were about to learn firsthand, the financial and time commitments required to care for and adopt out the dogs we had brought home.

We were more fortunate with this second group: only one young dog came down with parvo. Daisy was a white fur ball weighing about 12 lbs. In a shelter filled mostly with big dogs, she had stood out in the kennel runs, and Trulie had rationalized that a little, white dog should be easy to find a home for *and* wouldn't take up much room in the car. We were surprised when Daisy came down with parvo because we had heard that older dogs were less likely than puppies to become infected. The vets thought Daisy was still a youngster, so I questioned Trulie. But all Trulie knew for certain was that she had taken Daisy from the adult kennels. Daisy had a severe case of parvo and stayed at our local animal hospital for many days.

We were very worried that she wouldn't make it, but Daisy completely recovered and was soon adopted to a family who wanted a small, adult dog. Daisy is now a happy, fluffy 50 lb. dog! We often laugh at how little we knew in those days. Honestly though — seven years and thousands of dogs later — we are often surprised when families send pictures of dogs they adopted from us. When working with mixed breed puppies, you really never know their lineage.

Daisy provided us another example of the roller coaster ride our emotions can experience in rescue work. We were overjoyed at Daisy's victory over parvo, and sobered by the veterinary bills. We were still paying off our vet bills from the first rescue! About this time, we received our first and largest monetary donation. We put it towards our vet care expenses, and felt renewed. We were thankful for the money, and the donor's action was an encouraging reminder of how deeply other people care about the plight of homeless dogs.

We survived a huge learning curve in our first year. There was an amazing amount of work — and expenses to match — but we played a part in saving the lives of fifty-one dogs and puppies. We had lost two of our beautiful puppies to parvo, but the rest of our rescues were thriving and happy in their own homes, treasured members of a family. The roller coaster ride was worth it.

I had found my niche! I decided to establish my own independent rescue organization, and so I set up Lil' Waif Rescue. For several reasons, I decided to limit my rescue to puppies: bringing in older dogs was disruptive to my own dog's pack dynamics. And, quite honestly, I'm scared of dogs! I love them, but I'm not a natural dog person. I have a fear of big dogs, much to my daughters' chagrin. I'm comfortable with my own dogs, but even when puppies that I have had loved and cared for come back to visit as grown dogs, I often become nervous. I knew I had to focus my efforts on puppies.

Bigger Than We Planned

What a delight it was when we received our first incoming call for rescue assistance! A person from a well-established rescue group in Yakima wanted to know if we could help with a rescue and take some puppies. We were very excited: we had actually made it far enough that someone would call us in to assist! They informed us that we did not have to pay for the puppies, and wanted to know how many we could take. Ecstatic, we replied, "Bring what you can!"

We worked to be ready: setting up pens with crates, toys and blankets, with food and water dishes ready. We were prepared – at least I thought we were.

Unfortunately, I had to work the day the puppies were delivered. I was anxious to get home and meet the cute little puppies, and the eight hours I spent at work seemed long and tedious. Once home, I ran to our new makeshift puppy nursery. There were over twenty not-so-little puppies barking, howling, fighting, wetting and pooping.

Cozy Quarters: complete with warm blankets and lots of toys

We had never started with such big babies nor so many. We quickly realized that our nursery was more appropriate for very young puppies, not four-month-old puppies. We had no way to really contain them, so we sent them out into the yard to play. This meant two things: first, that our dogs would have to give up their yard and be taken out to be pottied on a leash. Second, and more importantly, we were taking a huge risk: parvo is common among puppies rescued from eastern Washington. If the puppies were contaminated with parvo, our yard could never again be used for puppies. Nevertheless, our yard was the only humane option.

We decided to move forward as quickly as possible and begin the task of identifying potential homes, in the hope that the puppies proved to be parvo-free. That day, we took pictures and paid extra so Evangelynn could quickly list the puppies on Petfinder®, and Dan started building a pen in the garage: this time, a taller and bigger pen.

That first incoming call for help had provided us further insight into the never ending

Lil'Waif's Puppy Rooms

learning curve. We had been excited to help all the puppies but naïve about how to set limits and what we really could accommodate. We now knew we needed to find ways to quarantine each litter until we were certain they were parvo-free and would not contaminate our yard. That call also marked the point at which we moved past begging for the opportunity to help save puppies. Soon, we were receiving calls from all over Washington: rescue organizations and private parties were asking us to take litters.

Once again, we found ourselves wondering how we were going to choose. It was the same painful dilemma we had encountered on our first shelter visit. How could we turn puppies away? How could we select some and leave others behind? We came to realize what all rescues eventually realize: we can't save them all. It had become clear on that day when we looked at the twenty big puppies running around in our very small yard: we needed to set rules and guidelines. If we wanted longevity as an active rescue organization, we couldn't continue making decisions based on impulse or emotional responses. Our set-up consisted of two bedrooms that held 5' x 5' pens and a very small, subdivision backyard for play. Those were limitations we could not change. We established our first rules: we would only take young puppy litters, six to eight weeks old, or younger if they no longer had a mother. Each litter needed to be quarantined and there could be no intermixing of litters until they had been vaccinated and in quarantine for ten days. This would contain any possible parvo. With these new guidelines in place, we felt that we were able to move on in rescue in a responsible way. The pain of turning away a litter or a needy dog has never diminished, but we know that our rescue has a specific purpose and calling. Knowing and respecting our limitations allows us to help the most dogs in the long run.

OUT OF THE BLUE

Meanwhile, Timmy was healing nicely. We had been together through surgery and physical therapy, and our bond was growing. I loved the way he looked at me with his big eyes. Our connection was the strongest I had felt with any dog. He was loving, sweet, smart and in my eyes just wonderful.

Unfortunately, life sometimes throws us a curve ball. This one came out of the blue when Timmy was nearly six months old. Evangelynn and I had taken our dogs to play fetch in a local park that we frequented. Timmy was a regular at that park: I had brought him there since the beginning – even when his cast was on we had gone there to enjoy the air. He loved the park and had always played nicely with the other dogs. On this day, something was different. A family had just ventured out to the park with a brand new Australian Shepherd puppy. When he saw them, Timmy's eyes took on a glazed, hollow look; something I had never seen before in my companion. Unfortunately, it was a look I was going to learn to recognize. With teeth bared, he took off running full speed towards the puppy. I ran after him, screaming for him to stop. There was no way for me to catch him. When I reached the scene, I found an angry man jerking Timmy off the innocent puppy. Timmy was in a complete state of arousal and continued trying to attack the puppy, now cowering on the ground. I was horrified, embarrassed and, honestly, confused. I tried to stutter apologies, but the man had no interest in hearing them, and I couldn't blame him. My dog had just terrorized his new puppy, probably on his first outing.

Trying to remember what to do, I took Timmy and firmly rolled him on his back; but by that point he was calm. He looked up at me submissively and lovingly. I was stymied as to what had triggered such a reaction from Timmy. Whatever it was, it seemed to be over. I was upset, but he really was just a sweet boy; my boy. I would be more vigilant with him off leash at the park. His leg was healing, and we were already signed up for basic obedience training. Whatever the problem was, I was sure we could work it out. However, whether I acknowledged it or not, a dark cloud was forming over my best friend, Timmy.

E.R.

We got a call, "Seven little puppies have been found. It seems they were dumped in the woods in eastern Washington. They're in bad shape: malnourished and full of ticks. Will you take them?" Ticks? We live in the Seattle area, where ticks are scarcely, if ever, seen. I hadn't had experience with them and didn't know how to remove them, so we quickly read everything we could find on the topic. The more I read, the more disgusted I became; but I decided that if I could deal with parvo and other puppy diseases, then surely I could remove a few ticks.

Alex, part of the feral pup crew

The puppies were brought to us by a volunteer, and I ran out to greet them. I thought I was prepared to handle my new challenge; however, one look at those babies and I almost fainted. There were possibly hundreds of ticks on each little body. With engorged ticks piled high one on top of another, you could not see inside the puppies' little ears. This was too much for me! We placed the babies back into a crate and headed for the vets. The office was closing for the night, and I wasn't even sure that I would be able to get them in.

Over the years I have worn a well-traveled path to the vet's office, each time holding a different puppy, each time wrought with worry. We have a couple of wonderful vets: each time I show up with my newest emergency they have managed to squeeze me in between their scheduled appointments. They have cared for and nurtured a number of my babies. I feel so fortunate to have such a working relationship with veterinarians

These two required one-in-a-million families, and both found them.

whom I trust! After pleading my case and seeing how distraught I was, my vet agreed to stay after and help. Once the staff saw the puppies, they too were appalled: everyone stayed to help alleviate the suffering of these little ones. Even with five helpers, Evangelynn and I spent two hours removing ticks one-by-one before we could declare our little ones "tick free." We were so thankful for all those caring hands that evening. We were sent home with lots of medicine and special foods to help build the puppies' immune systems. Those precious, tick-infested puppies grew to be strong, playful, sociable puppies, and in time all found loving homes.

A New Rescue Relationship

We had learned a lot as a new rescue, but time and time again we were plagued with parvo and other deadly puppy diseases. It took a toll on our finances and our emotions. We had to find a way to get to the puppies before they were infected. We now knew better than to ever take litters from shelters, as they just cannot control the rampant spread of disease. We decided that once the puppy hit the shelter door they were lost to us. We just couldn't risk it.

There are many differing opinions on how long parvo will stay active and contagious on your property, but the range is from months to years. We were playing with fire each time we had a breakout in our rescue. Many rescues have had to close down because their property became contagious, and we didn't want that to happen to us. At first, when we had a parvo puppy I would scour the pen, crate, bowls and toys with bleach and wash all the blankets with bleach. Then, despite hours of work I could not bring myself to take a chance on providing any of those items to other puppies. I gathered it all up and threw it all away, including the wood pen they had been housed in. This happened a few times before I could accept the difficult truth.

The best way I knew to keep puppies from being infected was to take in unwanted pregnant dogs and care for their litters from the beginning. It seemed like a good idea, but again I just couldn't find a way to bring a grown dog into my home. My daughter's dogs and Timmy were an established pack, I had a small yard, and I just didn't think it was plausible. I needed another solution.

About this time, a Yakima rescue that I had been working with offand-on had a change of leadership. With the changes, I was introduced to Shelley and Desi, both of whom were on the rescue's Board. I shared their vision for rescue, I admired their dedication and work, and I enjoyed their positive, upbeat personalities. We soon realized that maybe we could help each other out: I could handle puppies but not the mommy dogs. They were set up to foster adult dogs – including mommy dogs – but they had difficulty finding acceptable adoptive homes in their rural community. A friendship and rescue partnership was born.

Often it worked that Shelley or Desi would take in a pregnant dog (often a stray), whelp the litter, and keep them until they were weaned. Then, the babies would be transported to Lil' Waif. Our job was to care for them until we found the perfect home for each one. I had the advantage of having healthy and well-adjusted litters, while they had the advantage of knowing that each puppy they had cared for would go into the best of homes, as there is probably no one more particular than me when it comes to placing puppies! We all took pride in knowing that our working relationship rescued a litter from the hardships of being born into an environment they were unlikely to survive or, if they did survive, escape the life of a stray, which is often short and brutal. Each of the puppies we saved would be spayed or neutered; none of them would experience abuse or the loneliness of being a stray, and none would end up in a shelter like the one we had experienced at the start of our rescue.

This new working relationship was part of the solution to the bigger problem we were trying to solve, but what to do with litters that were born and then abandoned in the orchard or turned in by migrant workers who could not take puppies when they traveled? Both Shelley and Desi had situations where they had nice, sheltered kennels that worked great in all but the most extreme of weather. We would immediately give the puppies their shots and begin their ten-day quarantine period. We knew that if they did not show symptoms in ten days, they were clear. A solution had been found: I would be able to keep rescuing with my partners in Yakima without risk of bringing parvo into my rescue!

Since we have worked together, I have dealt with everything from broken limbs, blindness, unsocialized puppies and an assortment of other diseases, but we have staved off parvo.

SAVING LIL'THEO

What about Lil' Theodore, a precious little puppy that almost did not make it into rescue?

Shelley got one of those typical calls, "We have puppies. Come and get them, or we are going to dump them in the woods." Or sometimes it went, "Come and get them or we are going to shoot them." So Shelley headed out to retrieve another unwanted litter.

On these runs, Shelley and Desi often venture into areas far off the beaten path and meet people whose life circumstances barely provide a home for their family, let alone a family pet. When Shelley got to this site, the family handed her the puppies but said that the kids wanted to keep the littlest one. Shelley stood in front of their run-down home and watched as the kids passed it carelessly amongst themselves, often dropping it when it wiggled from their arms. Shelley tried to reason with them but

"Theodore"
Big name for a little fellow.

was unable to persuade them. She had no choice but to walk away and leave the puppy, though she felt sure the family could not afford to keep it and it would never be spayed or neutered. She felt frustrated and helpless; feelings that often haunt a rescuer. However, maybe because I was still so new at rescue and still so idealistic, I just couldn't give up. How could I take the litter knowing there was one still out there? I was worried for that little one's future, and what good did it do to take most of a litter but leave one only to breed more? We weren't accomplishing anything. I pleaded with Shelley to try again. Shelley now had to try to reason with me. "I did beg, and I tried to persuade them. But they were getting defensive, and I knew if I stayed any longer I would not get the ones I did get." Then I had an idea: what if we offered them money? I told Shelley I would reimburse her for whatever amount it took to "buy" the puppy from the family. I pleaded with her to go out and try one more time. Shelley returned to the run-down trailer, this time with her pockets full of cash, and started the negotiations with what she thought was a low offer.

"I will give you fifty dollars for that puppy," Shelley said.

The lady's eyes opened wide and she hollered to her son, "Go get that puppy. We just made fifty dollars!"

No one seemed to care that the puppy was leaving, and Shelley was relieved to find no broken bones in the little guy. This was not the last time I have sent either Shelley or Desi out with the instructions, "Whatever it takes, I want the whole litter. I will pay whatever it takes." It's not unusual for a family to give a litter to rescue but want to keep one or two of the cutest, or give one to a neighbor or some friend. These puppies, although novel for them at the moment, will end up running the streets un-neutered, or chained up just like their mother. We try everything in our arsenal to get people to consider the longer term; we will reason with them, threaten to not take the litter and then, as a last resort, we will offer to buy the puppies, at whatever cost. Often negotiations are difficult and tedious, further complicated if language barriers come into play. Despite the difficulties, we have two goals when taking a litter: first we take the whole litter, and second, we don't take a litter without also taking the mother dog into rescue or at the very least, paying to have her spayed. For that matter, if any other dogs live with the family, we cover the cost to spay or neuter them.

So little Theodore came into our rescue as our first "bought" puppy. I was in for a shock when I met Theodore a few days later. The rest of the puppies in the litter were of normal size, but this little puppy fit in the palm of our hands! We had housed runts before, but never one this small. This little guy needed a big and important name ... and we thought Theodore was appropriate!

We had no choice but to keep Theodore separate from his littermates, as they would run right over him and seemed to think he was a fun play toy.

We watched him grow from a little bit of a pup, to just a tad bigger of a puppy. Theodore was fast and could run around our couch in record time, blessing us with many good laughs. We will always remember Theodore as our very special, "little mister man."

Theodore now lives with a wonderful family and has a large yard, so he can zip around with those short but fast little legs as he runs those puppy victory laps. I know that I would have paid any amount of money to save this little guy.

FROM ORCHARD TO RESCUE

Two litters of feral pups were found together in an orchard, starving, cold and scared. The Yakima area's apple orchards, of which there are many, often become the dumping ground for unwanted litters. Several orchard rescues have come to us. Sometimes just a couple puppies are found, and we are left to wonder what happened to the rest of the litter. The most likely answer: coyotes. Did these little guys watch as their littermates were snatched by coyotes? Other times we find the rest

Sweet Nathaniel

of the litter frozen to death, or hit by passing cars on the nearby road. Maybe the saddest part about saving these dumped litters is that we have no opportunity to save the mother, bringing her into rescue or even just having her spayed. These mommas will continue to have litters, only to see their babies taken away from them, to be dumped in the nearest orchard or roadside ditch.

These two particular litters were extremely feral acting; very shy and scared. They didn't want to be touched and cowered in the back of the pens. They obviously had never been handled or exposed to humans. Many litters don't get the appropriate socialization that puppies need but are able to come around quickly with a little attention, but these litters were different. The typical reaction of puppies to me entering the room is for them to run to the front of the pen, jump up and cry to be held ... but not these guys ... they would run to the back of the pen, hide their heads and shake. Two litters of very unsocial puppies took us to an entirely different and unfamiliar challenge! These puppies needed lots and lots of time and attention to learn how to trust humans.

Some need extra time to learn how to be loved.

My husband, Dan, and I did what we could. We spent hours sitting in their pens with them, quietly reassuring them. However, we both had to work and keep other commitments; we just could not give them all the time they needed to learn how to trust. I was distressed that we would never be able to get them to a point where they could be adoptable, and we had so many of them! Someone suggested that I put a note on the bulletin board of a nearby well-known company, asking people to come and sit with these puppies. I thought about it, but was hesitant about strangers coming into my house to volunteer, and decided against it. However, someone, who to this day remains a mystery person, took the initiative and posted a notice at a prominent, local software company. Our phone began ringing non-stop, and our front door became a revolving door with caring volunteers. Often groups of four or five volunteers would come. We spread out tarps on our living room carpet so there would be plenty of wall-to-wall space to sit and play with puppies. The puppies were saturated with love and attention, and had no choice but to start trusting humans and learn how to love back. Slowly, they did so. They never became exuberant, but they were all able to grow to a place where they could be adopted out to families who love them, and whom they love and trust in return. These once feral pups were truly loved and cared for by a village.

HOLDING ONTO HOPE

Puppy rescue was going well, and Timmy and I were having a blast. Timmy definitely brought out the best in me. We had started with basic obedience classes and then moved to other classes, such as Rally Obedience, where the handler and dog navigate a series of obstacles and directions on a timed course. We also had enrolled in a tricks class. Tim was a quick learner, and I was starting to feel confident as a trainer, something that was new to me. I had grown up with farm dogs, and my daughters had dogs that they acquired as adults, but Timmy was the first dog that was really mine; that I trained. People assumed that because I did puppy rescue I was an accomplished trainer and/or savvy with dogs. Nothing could be further from the truth! The truth was I was a complete novice, and dog training was moving me way beyond my comfort zone. However, together Timmy and I were finding success and learning to work smoothly as a team. We both cherished our training time together and our bond only continued to grow. We were even learning freestyle dancing, and we both loved it. I was sure that Timmy was going to be my dancing partner for life.

In the car, ready to roll.

As long as Timmy was totally focused on me, all was well. Problems were brewing, though, and I could sense it. In class, I had to be very diligent to keep his attention at all times. If his eyes strayed to another dog I could sense his nervousness. I shared my concerns with a couple of instructors, seeking advice. But I always received the same response, "What? Timmy? Oh, he's not a problem dog!" These were instructors whom I trusted and who had a lot of experience with dogs … and so I decided to ignore that twinge of worry I felt.

Then, one day in an obedience class, Timmy attacked another dog. We had been walking, with everyone heeling in a circle. Timmy was walking nicely next to me, his eyes on me, when suddenly – without any warning that I could sense – he turned and lunged at the dog behind us. I yanked Timmy off, and with a great deal of struggle was able to walk him to the corner of the room to try to calm him. The instructor came over and, in an attempt to comfort me, said, "That may not have been

Timmy's fault. You don't know what message the dog behind him was sending." I saw the other dog owner's jaw drop when he heard that! He was quite visibly upset. I mouthed to him, "I'm sorry," but he just stared in disbelief. I doubted we would see him in class again.

Sharing a big grin.

I started realizing that maybe our instructors were blinded by Timmy's big brown eyes and sweet disposition, and that we needed more professional help.

I didn't realize the extent of the journey I was embarking on in search of an answer to Timmy's problems.

We began to theorize as to what may be the issue. Sometimes Timmy would do clumsy things like fall off the side of the sidewalk. Maybe the issue was that Timmy could not see clearly and his limited vision prompted him to act as he did. We saw an animal ophthalmologist, but as far as the doctor could tell his eyes were fine. They could only look for astigmatism though; they really couldn't get a feel for his overall vision.

Timmy's leg had never healed properly, and it was short and thin. Maybe it was causing him pain, which in turn was causing him to act out. We made an appointment with an orthopedic surgeon. Sure enough, we learned that his leg could be causing him pain because scar tissue was wrapped around the metal plate in his leg. The surgeon said that an operation would not solve the problem, but he suggested we try acupuncture; it could relieve Timmy's pain and

Timmy with his older dog sibling, Holly.

calm him down. Timmy loved his acupuncture sessions and would always fall asleep during treatment; however, his tension around other dogs remained, and he would at times yelp in pain when running or playing.

As if that wasn't enough, Timmy seemed to be developing another affliction: allergies. Some mornings Timmy would rub his eyes on the carpet until they looked raw and bloodshot. Maybe the allergies were the cause of his aggression. Perhaps the miseries of the symptoms of allergies were affecting him more than we knew. Dan and I took Timmy into Seattle to see a very highly recommended animal allergist. As Timmy lay sprawled across our laps in his typical fashion (he always thought he was a lapdog) we discussed Timmy's symptoms with the doctor. The doctor ran many tests, and the results showed that Timmy was allergic to many things. Most significant was his allergy to the dust mite. On that test his reading was a ten, indicating the highest sensitivity on the scale.

Timmy on the patio, his picnic table throne.

Dust mites in the environment are just about impossible to control, so we started Timmy on a series of shots. I learned to administer them and gave him his shots daily. Despite my hopefulness and diligence, there seemed to be no improvement in either his allergies or his fits of aggression.

We decided to look at professional dog trainers in hopes that their training would give us the direction we needed to curb his aggression. Maybe we just didn't know how to properly train Timmy. If we learned the correct methods, we might be able to rid him of his issues. A professional dog trainer was recommended to us, so we made an appointment for her to come to our house. She wanted to test Timmy's level of dog aggression herself, so she placed her own dog in her car with the window cracked open a couple of inches and walked Timmy back and forth and around the car to measure Timmy's reaction. Timmy had no reaction, despite the dog barking at him. I was starting to feel like my concern was unsubstantiated. She turned to me, and was asking me what exactly I thought the problem was when Timmy suddenly charged the car, attacking the window. Her dog squealed in fright and jumped away from the window. The trainer, who had been caught off guard, was pulled over with Timmy's sudden charge. She threw Timmy to the pavement and held him there. He seemed to come out of his state as quickly as he went into it, and now was scared and whimpering. Being the incredibly sensitive dog Timmy was, he was shaken for a long time afterward. Perhaps the worst part was that I knew that she had hurt Timmy's leg. We always tried so hard to protect it and keep him from straining it, but when she flipped him over his leg was twisted. I knew this method was not going to work for us, and this trainer was definitely not going to work for us. I understood the concept of asserting dominance and being the pack leader, but except for sudden and unexpected bursts of aggression, Timmy never showed a bit of dominance, either to us or the other dogs in the house. He was sweet and compliant, actually quite submissive. However, we took the advice of the trainer: we stopped allowing him on furniture and limited other privileges. We grieved our nightly cuddle sessions on the couch, but if this would help we would follow through; and we quickly found the floor to be just as inviting.

L<small>IVE</small>, L<small>OVE AND</small> S<small>MILE</small>

Little Luke came to us with his litter. Immediately we noticed something was wrong with this little guy's gait. As Luke grew it became apparent he had growth abnormalities: his front legs were growing crooked.

The vets said the only thing they could do for him was to wrap his legs in a way that might encourage them to grow evenly. His legs were wrapped, and we were instructed to keep Luke quiet and contained. This proved to be a fairly difficult task, because

Puppy Luke

Luke did not allow his special needs to deter him from having an enthusiastic puppyhood. He greeted us each day with love and kisses. He had boundless energy! We loved little Luke, but who else would love this little black puppy with crooked legs? Who were we going to find to love him?

*Time to play! Luke and his big sister doing what dogs do best.
Luke's legs do not hold him back from play.*

Luke's happy ending always makes us smile. An injured Vietnam War veteran was looking for a walking buddy, a companion that would enjoy life but stroll at his pace. Luke now walks daily on the beach with his dad. He is loved and loves life. He and his dad are inspirations, never letting their physical disability get in the way of their living full and loving lives.

BUNNIES? NO. PUPPIES IN A BASKET.

Easter of 2003 was a memorable day for me. As a mother and grandmother, I was excited to have my daughter Beth, her husband Scott and my only grandchild, three-year-old Amanda, staying with me for a short visit. I had everything planned: the Easter meal, coloring eggs, and my personal favorite – attending the local Basset Hound Parade.

It had been a very cold and unpredictable spring. The weather reports that Easter alerted travelers to the spring storm that had just moved in over Washington State. Snoqualmie Pass, the main route over the mountains between eastern and western Washington, was closed and there were many stranded travelers. I was thankful that my family members were safe and cozy with me.

We were just getting ready to sit down to our Easter dinner when the phone rang. Shelley was on the line. She informed me that she had received a phone call from a hysterical woman whose drunken husband had blown the head off her black Labrador Retriever, and the woman was afraid he would next hurt the nursing babies.

Puppies take refuge at Lil'Waif for all kinds of reasons.

"I'm on my way out there right now to try to save the babies," Shelley said. "Could you meet me at the Summit?"

Shelley already had a litter she was bottle-feeding and could not manage two litters. "The Summit is closed," I told her, but she assured me that it opened periodically and we could pull this off. Shelley was venturing into dangerous territory, a drunken man with a gun. I worried for her safety, but she was determined to save the babies.

Scott volunteered to drive, and Beth and Evangelynn threw their coats on to go with him. I looked at my family. A moment before they had been relaxing contentedly, cozy and warm. Now they were getting ready to travel on treacherous roads, and my holiday dinner was already getting cold. I stayed behind with my granddaughter and spent my time praying.

From start to finish, the whole mission could not have gone smoother. When Shelley reached the house of the drunken man, he was sleeping. She was able to collect the puppies and leave without him noticing. The Summit re-opened in such a way that it provided a textbook example of the phrase "perfect timing!" Shelley was able to meet up with Scott and the girls and hand over the puppies. Three hours later, I again had my family with me, plus five little black labs.

How irresistible they were!

I knew that ahead of me lay weeks of bottle feeding the precious puppies every couple hours, day and night, but my heart was happy. I was deeply grateful that the puppies were safe. I could enjoy the rest of the holiday.

I was so proud of my family; they were a part of me and now shared a part of rescue.

SEARCHING FOR SHELTER

It seems that old, abandoned houses are a haven for stray, pregnant, female dogs. The house may be infested and falling down, but to a mom about to give birth it represents shelter for her and her soon-to-be-born pups. So it is that old, abandoned houses also seem to attract rescue workers. Often, you can find Shelley and other brave rescuers checking out the remnants of some forsaken house. One particularly cold night just before nightfall, Shelley called me on her cell phone from such a site.

"I found a litter of puppies underneath this old shack. I've crawled under the house with my flashlight, and I see them! I don't know what to do. If I take the babies, the momma will run away and we won't be able to catch her. She needs a home too, and she needs to be spayed. If I leave the puppies here, they will freeze. I already see a couple of dead ones."

My first concern was Shelley. "Shelley, are you safe?"

She didn't really know. She was trying her best not to move anything that would make the old house collapse, and it was too dark to know who or what else was really under that old shack. Yes, she was scared, but what was she to do?

"Shelley, you need to call someone to tell them where you are. You don't want to get stuck under there. No one knows your location!"

"Yeah, yeah, I will. But what do I do about the babies? They are very afraid and ran to the far corner. I can't reach them."

"Get out, Shelley, that's what you do! You get out!" I reasoned with her. "You can go back in the morning, with some help."

Shelley, always ready for emergencies, threw blankets under the house and left a bag of dog food for the momma.

The next morning, bright and early, Shelley was back at the old deserted house with her sister, Denise. They searched and searched for the momma, but she wasn't to be found. She was either hiding or had abandoned her litter once she knew that their hiding place had been discovered.

Shelley went to work. She would shimmy under the house, throw a towel over a puppy, gently wrap it, shimmy back out and hand Denise the bundled-up pup. Denise then carefully placed the pup in the warm car, while Shelley worked her way under the house to save another pup.

After the fifth puppy was safely in the car, Shelley crawled around under the old house just to make sure there wasn't a puppy that had been missed. Once she was satisfied that she had found all the live puppies, five little yellow fur balls were on their way to Lil' Waif!

Shelley left food and water, but the momma dog did not return. It was inevitable that she would soon have another litter, maybe even under the same house. All Shelley could do was watch for her, and that she would do. Shelley does not give up easily.

AN OLD ABANDONED HOUSE

"Rebecca, I'm at this old deserted house!" I heard Shelley's voice at the other end of the phone.

Where had I heard that before?

"There's a momma and daddy dog with seven babies. I got here just in time! The babies are a little young to wean, but I think the momma's milk is dry and they are all starving. The father is nice but is concerned, and he's standing guard over the momma and babies. If I can lure him out, I can get to the others."

Here we go again, I thought. "Shelley, who is with you in case the daddy dog becomes aggressive? You are putting yourself in a very dangerous situation with no back-up."

"Oh, I'm okay. I need to get these guys help! After I get them, will you take the puppies? There are two really small runts that will need middle of the night feedings. Can you meet me at the Summit in about two hours? We have to get these babies warm and fed."

Shelley has a natural way with dogs, and with patience and some liver treats was able to win over the heart of the male dog. Soon, she had the family in her car. The mother dog, feeling like so many feral dogs do when rescued, seemed relieved to have help with her puppies. As soon as Shelley began caring for them, the momma dog relaxed.

We reached the Summit and found Shelley waiting for us, anxious that the puppies get settled and drink some much-needed nourishment. The two smallest ones fit comfortably in the palms of our hands and were almost lifeless, while the other five puppies were rather big and robust. Once home, we put the babies in their new, clean pen and immediately the biggest puppy (who we ended up naming Teddy because he resembled a big, white, fluffy teddy bear) picked up the littlest runt in his mouth and ran in a circle around the pen, throwing his little sister up in the air like a miniature stuffed animal.

By the time I had fed the puppies their goat's milk, Dan had built a new, small pen to keep the littlest ones safe from the enthusiasm of their big brother, Teddy. We named our little ones, JuJu and JoJo and prayed they would make it. Even the most attentive nursing cannot guarantee success, and there were many times during the next few days when I thought JuJu and JoJo might be taking their last breaths. My niece, Laurie, kept sending me encouraging e-mails and praying non-stop for the puppies' health. Eventually, both pups started to turn around and show some spark.

JuJu and JoJo are now full-grown dogs. They are still small, but they have large and playful personalities. Shelley, Dan, Laurie and I had worked together to earn a priceless reward: health and well-being for these two vulnerable creatures.

Clockwise from upper left: Momma dog Jill, Daddy dog Jack,
JuJu and JoJo

The Canine Clampetts

Shadows in the woods ... Michelle spotted them one cold, winter morning while working at the apple packing factory in Yakima Valley.

On the edge of the orchard, living in the bordering woods, was a small pack of feral dogs. Michelle observed them for several days. She thought there were three – no four, or maybe more. It was hard to say for sure: the black-and-tan dogs looked identical and skittered in and out of the reaches of the woods.

Michelle attempted to approach them, offering them delicious smelling morsels of food. They stood their distance, watching her with curiosity until she breached some invisible boundary, at which point they bolted into the woods. Those environs must have felt like a safety zone to the pack, but it was obvious that the dogs were unable to adequately forage and hunt among the frozen winter woods. They all appeared to be starving. Michelle noted that one of them seemed to be struggling to keep up with the pack: he had a severe limp and appeared to be in pain. And, one of the females appeared to be pregnant. Michelle grew more determined than ever to help this family of feral dogs.

Michelle called Desi, a long-time dog rescuer and friend of Shelley's. Together they discussed strategies for rescuing this forlorn pack. There was the issue of actually catching the dogs and then the bigger issue of what to do with them once they had them. Who could take in or care for five feral, adult dogs? It was a dilemma, but it didn't stop either Michelle or Desi. Michelle continued to work on gaining the dogs' trust, visiting them daily with food. She focused on the one with the injured leg. There may have been a time when he had been able to fend for himself, hunting and scrounging for food, but he was now weak and getting thinner. At last came the day when he approached her, compelled by the smell of the food. He made it all the way to Michelle before he collapsed, right into her arms. Michelle scooped him up and rushed him to the vet hospital, where he received all the medical treatment he required, including the setting of his broken leg.

Michelle and Desi were thrilled to have the little guy safe and sound. It did not go unnoticed that he would not have survived one more day in the woods before suffering death from cold and starvation. Michelle's first rescue, now named Mickey, was less thrilled. For the first time he was in a house, away from his pack, and he had a cast on his leg. He was very, very frightened. He found a spot behind a toilet in a small bathroom and planted himself there, obviously wary of humans. Desi was patient, letting him have his spot and giving him all the time and space he needed to learn that he was safe. On his own, Mickey started venturing out to seek and accept the attention and love offered by the people beyond the bathroom door.

As happy as Desi and Michelle were to have been able to help Mickey, they were distressed by the fact that four hungry, cold dogs – one of them obviously pregnant – were still roaming the woods beyond the orchard. Calls were made, and eventually a local animal control organization offered to lend them a humane dog trap. The trap was a large crate with a spring-activated door; once an animal entered the crate, the door would close to prevent their exit. Michelle camouflaged the crate with apple boxes, and placed it where she could see it through her window at work. There was a lot of excitement and hope with the trap in place. I know that I probably called on the hour, every hour with the same question: "Anything yet?" Eventually, I heard a "yes."

Mickey, learning to love, beyond the bathroom tile floor.

Sierra was the first to succumb to the temptation of the bacon placed strategically in the trap. Poor Sierra, I am sure she thought the worst had just happened. Sierra's pregnancy was obvious and Desi had her hands full with Mickey and other fosters, so Sierra was placed in Shelley's care. It worked out well – Desi wouldn't have puppies to care for on top of everything else – but Sierra, like Mickey, was not so sure at first. She was scared and wary of humans. Shelley worked to gain her trust, and in time Sierra came to understand that food and love come from caring people.

One-by-one the other three were trapped in succession, and rather quickly. Hector, Sienna and Pluto all succumbed to the temptation by bacon and were caught in the trap, then taken to Desi's kennel. Now what? It had taken weeks to coax all of these guys to safety. Desi fed and watered them and cleaned up after them, but she was careful not to impose on them by touching them or making eye contact. We began to call the pack the Clampett family, after the TV show, The Beverly Hillbillies. It seemed appropriate, since they all had gone suddenly from subsistence hunting (squirrels for dinner) to living the easy life.

The dogs were kenneled together and continued to depend on each other as a group. They were all very wary of people and would cower at the back of the kennel when anyone approached. Progress was slow, but Desi knew they were beginning to accept her when they started greeting her at the front of the kennel.

The day came when Desi felt that the Clampetts were acclimated and adjusted well enough to be allowed out of the kennel. When she let them out, the gang ran and played freely until they were tired and hungry. Then, together, they went back into the kennel and barked until the door was shut behind them. They felt secure if they were protected from the outside world. Thus a new routine was started. They were let out of their kennel to run and enjoy the property during the day, then returned to their safe kennel in the evening, happy to have the door shut behind them. Each day they were starting to accept and trust Desi more.

That summer, Desi and her family vacationed for a week, leaving a house sitter to watch over the Clampetts and the other foster dogs. The first time the sitter opened the kennel door for them to have their daily romp, the Clampetts bolted and disappeared. The sitter looked and looked but could not find them. When they failed to come back, she called Desi. Desi's week of planned relaxation with her family turned into an anxious week, largely spent counting down the time until she could return home and search for her "Clampett Gang." When Desi's family finally pulled into the driveway from their vacation, and she stepped out of the van, three lonely, hungry dogs emerged from the woods. They had obviously been staying just beyond the tree line, where they had been watching and waiting for her. Desi was home, and the Clampetts felt safe again.

Meanwhile, by the time his cast was removed, Mickey had become a friendly and well-adjusted house dog. He needed physical therapy. Fortunately, Desi has a swimming pool. Three times daily, she undertook the monotonous task of providing therapy for his healing leg. Soon

enough, Mickey was well enough to be adopted: now he has his very
own boy who loves him, limp and all.

Mickey, and his therapy pool — comfortable in his new surroundings.

Sierra (who had adjusted nicely to Shelley's pack of dogs made up of
her own rescues and fosters) gave birth to nine robust black puppies in
the spring. Only two weeks later, Sienna, who was less than a year old,
gave birth to six black puppies. So much for the plan of placing Sierra
with Shelley so Desi would not have to add puppy care to her schedule!
Both girls were good mommies, and all fifteen puppies thrived.

Without the intervention of caring rescuers, would any of these
puppies have survived the cold and coyotes? Possibly a few, but what
kind of life would they have led? Most likely, a life like their mothers had
led in the wild – starving, cold, pregnant or impregnating, and distrust-
ful of people. We were so thankful for each little one!

Lil' Waif had fifteen identical, black, furry little ones to love, care
for and place into loving homes. Each one was special and deserving …
but fifteen of them? How were we ever going to find homes for all fifteen? The task seemed daunting. The litters had arrived as summer was

beginning, one of our slowest times. Evangelynn and I reconsidered our extremely stringent adoption requirements and decided that it would be necessary to ease up if we were going to find homes for all of them. We told ourselves that at least they would be sheltered, fed and neutered. Maybe that was the best we could do. It was a good thought, but somehow when we got those "pretty good" applications we just couldn't bring ourselves to follow up on them. Each of those puppies was as deserving as any other puppy. We wanted them to have the best. Despite Trulie's teasing about us ending up with fifteen big dogs running around the puppy yard, we held out for the perfect application for each puppy. And, just like their wild relatives who one by one were brought to safety, one by one each puppy found their loving home and family.

I bet you are wondering where the Clampetts are today. It has been two years now, and Pluto, Sienna and Hector continue to live with Desi. They have made huge strides: Pluto now sleeps under the bed, Sienna plays the role of surrogate mother to all the foster puppies, and Hector finally learned that he doesn't have to run when visitors come: he can just watch from a distance. Desi already had three dogs of her own and did not intend to bring in three more … but what is a rescuer to do?

Rags to riches … Pluto, Hector and Sienna

An Unlikely Duo

Her little body flew through the air, tossed from the car as it raced down the freeway. No one knows what her life had been like or why she was disposed of like unwanted trash on the highway, but it was this seemingly traumatic moment in little Mischa's life that was the catalyst for her finding help and love through a rescue.

Mischa's first angel was in the form of the person who witnessed her being tossed from the car and stopped to help her.

Shelley opened her door one rainy night to a sobbing lady who was holding Mischa, a wet, skinny pit bull. Shelley became Mischa's next angel. She took her in, cleaned her and gave her a full examination. She was relieved to find no broken bones, but Mischa's body had no hair and was pink and raw all over. Despite having been cleaned, she had a repulsive odor emanating from her. Shelley stayed awake most of that night trying to comfort Mischa, who was traumatized and miserable.

The next morning, Shelley was waiting on the doorstep of the vets when they unlocked their doors. Mischa's skin was bright red, with terrible open sores and road burn. The odor was a yeast infection, and the loss of hair was due to mange. Shelley's list of daily dog chores grew to include giving shots every day for two weeks and baths with special shampoos every other day.

Mischa thrived on the love at Shelley's house and soon picked a new best friend from among the other resident dogs. Sierra (the only dog from the Clampett gang to have been placed at Shelley's) had weaned her puppies and was slowly making progress in her socialization. She was still shy and very wary of people. Sierra and Mischa, once the outcasts of the dog world, united as a team. Together these two could win over every situation, and win they did. Mischa's skin became smooth as silk, and beautiful soft hair grew in where before it had been red and irritated. Sierra was no longer scared with gentle Mischa by her side. These two were inseparable, bonded for life. Shelley, who had witnessed this special bond, asked if we could find them a home together.

While Shelley was holding out hope, truthfully, I doubted we would be able to place either one. Every year, so many beautiful, well-adjusted dogs are euthanized in shelters due to lack of homes: how were we going to find a home for a dog as shy as Sierra? And pit bulls are always difficult to place in the right home. Laurie, my niece, promised to pray for a miracle. Evangelynn did her best by putting pictures of the duo on the website, alongside her touching description of their love for each other. I continually reminded everyone that we needed to be thankful if we could place each one in a good home individually, as the chances of finding them a home together was unlikely. Meanwhile, Shelley continued to foster the girls, and Sierra and Mischa continued to enjoy life together.

Mischa

Then came the day we got the inquiry: someone had seen the pictures of the two playing on Petfinder® and was interested in both girls. I sent an application and tried not to get my hopes up. The couple responded quickly, and I could not believe my eyes. I read the application several times, thinking I must be missing something. A retired couple living on a horse ranch in western Washington wanted to adopt two dogs together and was interested in our Sierra and Mischa. Could it be any more perfect? There had to be a catch.

The catch? Only my reluctance to believe that another rescue miracle would occur! Mischa and Sierra now live a pampered life, and love life – together!

Sierra

The girls living out every rescue dog's dream: Finding a family to call their own.

Mischa at home on the ranch.

SHERIFF OF DOGTOWN

A dog-loving sheriff like Roy is a bonus for any community, but for Yakima he is a special entity. Yakima and Seattle are a mere two and a half hour drive from each other, but they are as different as separate planets. A litter of puppies found in the woods of western Washington will make the six o'clock news. The following night the news will follow up with the story of how authorities were able to track down the people who abandoned the puppies and file criminal charges. In eastern Washington there is no legal recourse for even the most atrocious acts of abuse on animals, and litters are abandoned on a regular basis. Roy, however, was always concerned about the dogs in the community and would often call Desi with news of strays or abandoned puppies. He would often meet and assist her in rescue missions, helping to capture a stray or collect a litter of abandoned puppies.

One cold snowy night, Roy called Desi to see if she would accompany him to a home where he had seen a couple of dead puppies out on the road. The puppies had obviously wandered out onto the busy road and been struck. Roy was not sure what he would find, but he certainly expected to find more puppies and hoped Desi would take them.

Neither Roy nor Desi were prepared for the horrible reality. It was many nights before Desi was able to shut her eyes without reliving the nightmare.

When they arrived at the house near the site, they found the front door wide open and a disabled man sitting on the couch staring at a blaring TV. There was garbage everywhere. The man could not communicate in any way, nor did he even acknowledge their presence. Roy and Desi walked into the backyard to find the most hideous situation: there were five big, mangy dogs chained up. Some seemed friendly, some not. All were cold, thin and living without food or shelter. Puppies were lying about the yard, some barely alive, some dead. Desi made the mistake of kicking a lump in the snow: it was a dead dog. There were dog skeletons everywhere. How long had dogs been chained and starved to death in this yard? How many dogs had died in this tormented graveyard?

Roy and Desi knew there wasn't much they could do for the adult dogs until the local shelter and Animal Control opened the next morning. Getting the puppies into a safe environment was their first priority. They poured out food, and gave water to the starving adults, then gathered the live puppies. Roy would return with help in the morning.

Unfortunately, when Roy returned in the morning, he found many of the dogs had been unchained and were gone, probably let loose to continue the all-too-familiar cycle of starvation and pregnancy.

"OH, YOU DO PUPPY RESCUE? HOW FUN TO PLAY WITH PUPPIES ALL DAY!"

Desi called me, still traumatized by her horrific experience. Some of the puppies had died, but there were still three very sick little ones. The puppies had been checked by a veterinarian and shots and antibiotics had been administered, but they were ill with pneumonia and kennel cough, and their little bodies were very malnourished. We had nursed puppies many times before, so we knew that we could accept this challenging task. Dan built a new pen in the mudroom hallway to prevent the kennel cough from spreading to our regular pens, and the three puppies – Jolie, Jeremiah, and Joey – came to Lil' Waif. They coughed day and night. As they fought for their lives, we found ourselves holding our breath, fearing their next breaths would be their last.

While listening to our three J's cough, we heard the phone ring. Three little pit bull mixes had been saved by someone who had witnessed them being terrorized by teenagers in the neighborhood. The hairless pups had sarcoptic mange, which is extremely contagious to

Left to right: Jolie, Jeremiah, Joey

other dogs. Dan set to work building a pen in an empty bedroom, distant from the puppy room and the mudroom hallway.

The next few weeks, our daily operations seemed as complex as those at any hospital. We had to be sure that Jolie, Jeremiah and Joey were not exposed to mange, that the pit bull boys were not exposed to kennel cough, and that the other puppies and our own dogs were not exposed to either. To eliminate cross contamination, Evangelynn cared for the "3 J's" and I cared for the pit bull boys. I would strip my clothes before leaving the room, and before and after any contact with our little patients, we all scrubbed our hands and arms like surgeons.

I gave the pit bull puppies daily medication and baths with special shampoo, and I spent hours each day reassuring them that their future held nothing but love and fun. Despite the tender loving care, my boys were made miserable by the sarcoptic mange. They continuously scratched. Twenty-four hours a day we could hear the thump-thump-thump of their feet hitting the floor as they scratched. We went to bed at night and worked during the day to the tune of coughing and thumping. I felt helpless, but I knew that in a short time these precious boys would not remember the itchiness of sarcoptic mange, and they would never again experience torture from humans.

Meanwhile, in our puppy room we had healthy puppies! Four of them were one-week-old babies that had been found in a box on the steps of a Yakima courthouse in the middle of winter. These pup-

pies needed hand feeding. Since Evangelynn was tending the kennel cough pups and I was caring for the mange boys, Dan and a few friends took responsibility for feeding Mindy, Samuel, Davey and Leah first with an eyedropper, then with a bottle every couple hours.

Mindy   *Samuel*

Christmas came and went. There wasn't a Christmas tree, there weren't presents to put under a Christmas tree, there wasn't a Christmas dinner ... we had neither time nor energy. This was not our first holiday that was lost and forgotten in the busyness of caring for orphan puppies, nor would it be the last. This was probably not what we had envisioned when we started puppy rescue. I think we had envisioned lots of hours playing with puppies, and maybe nursing the occasional few back to health. Maybe it's best we didn't anticipate the nights without sleep, absence of social life, tears of disappointment, and complaints from neighbors when the puppies are barking. We are rewarded, though, with each wonderful adoption, knowing that another little friend will live a full and love-filled life.

FADING HOPE

Timmy was progressing, but not for the better. No one – not dog instructors, friends or strangers – any longer saw Timmy as a sweet, innocent dog. I imagined that in their heads they had swapped the image of Timmy with a halo over his head to that of Timmy with horns. This only made me more protective of Timmy and more determined to help him.

Our classes in training, tricks and freestyle dancing were no longer an option, due to Timmy's unpredictable behavior around other dogs. I missed going to classes with Timmy and working together as a team in a group. We continued to work together at home, but it wasn't the same. Another issue was arising. We were beginning to struggle with how to get Timmy exercised every day. I had a strong commitment to exercise Timmy on a very regular basis. I believe most behavior issues with dogs come from lack of exercise. Timmy had been an active, busy puppy and young dog. I knew he needed his outings, just like the other dogs, but his behavior restricted our scope. Evangelynn and I would take Timmy out to a small wooded area early in the morning, before anyone else would think about crawling out of their warm beds. She would go to one side of the woods, and I would go to the other. Timmy would then run from one to the other, jumping over tree trunks and splashing in puddles, always rewarded for his short journey with a piece of cheese. Timmy never tired of this daily exercise and always enjoyed whatever simple pleasures we could give him, endearing him even more to our hearts.

One day, we wanted to take all of our dogs swimming at a local dog park that Timmy had enjoyed when he was younger. We decided to try taking Timmy once again. Timmy was muzzled, and I had a pocket full of his favorite cheese. I was hoping we would have a positive experience: Shortly after we arrived, Timmy went after a small dog in his aggressive way. I was close by, and he was muzzled so there was no damage, but I was deeply disappointed that we couldn't even take him swimming or to our favorite dog park without him acting up. Then, Timmy spotted a young dog romping around not too far from him. Timmy turned towards me with fear in his eyes and came tearing towards me in a dead panic. When he got to me, he hid behind me and shook, which he continued to do for the rest of the morning. His behavior was so inconsistent between aggression and fear! Perhaps all the aggression was based on a deep fear of other dogs. Maybe having his leg broken so young, and being in pain among his littermates had made him fearful of other dogs. I didn't know why he acted the way he did, nor did I know how to help him. Our dog park adventure was short: we loaded the dogs back into the car, where Timmy anxiously drooled on the ride home, soaking his towels and me. No more dog parks for Timmy, just early morning romps in our neighborhood woods.

Our early morning outings came to an end due to another incident. As diligent as I tried to be, one morning a dog came running out of the woods unexpectedly. Timmy was startled and charged the dog, with his fangs bared. Timmy did not respond to my calls. It turned into a moment of pure panic, where everything seemed to happen in slow motion but I was helpless to stop it from happening. The dog tried to get away, but Timmy went after him. If the dog's owner had not been there, I'm not sure what would have happened. The dog ran back to his person, who grabbed Timmy and pulled him off his own dog. I collected Timmy, embarrassed and humiliated again. The man said that Timmy had no business being out there, and I knew he was right. My attempts at keeping him away from other dogs by going out so early was just too risky. I knew that was the last time that Timmy was going to be able to play off leash. I wished I had a spot for him to really romp at home, but our backyard was small, and most of it was taken up with puppy play pens.

Timmy enjoyed leashed walks, but even they were problematic. One day we walked out our front door and, before I saw it, Timmy spotted a dog wandering near our front yard. He went into one of his rages, lunging and straining against the leash. I knew I could not let go, but Timmy was strong and pulled me down the stairs face first. As soon as he saw what he had done he immediately became upset and worried. He stood over me, whimpering and shaking. I was scratched and dirty, and my pants and shirt were ripped. When I walked back into the house a very surprised Evangelynn came running. "Mom, Mom! What happened? Are you all right? Here, sit down, Mom, sit here!"

I assured Evangelynn I was all right but very shaken and did appreciate the chair being offered to me, as my legs were very wobbly. Timmy laid his head on my lap and whined. He knew he had hurt me, and I could tell he felt bad. Timmy kept looking at me with his eyes, which said, "I'm so sorry," and loving me with his furry head. I knew he regretted hurting me; however it also confirmed to me that when he was in that state, he had no control over his actions. How would he have felt if he had really hurt me? That was something I didn't want him to have to live with either.

Initially I thought I was just scratched and bruised, but my pain became intense. A doctor visit and a casted broken arm later, I knew Timmy couldn't safely be taken for leash walks. I began to really worry about Timmy's quality of life. He was loved dearly, but he was miserable with allergies that often left his eyes bloodshot, and now he was under house arrest. I didn't know what to do … where was I going to find help for Timmy?

I got another dog behaviorist referral. We were told that she was expensive, but good. I made the appointment and went with the thought that I needed just the smallest amount of encouragement that Timmy could be helped. Evangelynn and I sat in the waiting room with Timmy, who paced and drooled. It seemed even visits to the vet's office were becoming an excruciating ordeal for Timmy. While the behaviorist asked us questions during our session, she watched Timmy. I wished Timmy would stop and just relax a little, but I was incapable of getting him to calm down. In the end, the doctor gave us some exercises and some lilac scent to plug into the wall for a calming effect, but her main recommendation was Prozac. It seemed to be a high dosage, and I was concerned. It was when I was questioning her on the dosage that I heard the words: "Timmy," she said, " … is the most neurotic dog I have ever observed."

Surely Timmy was not the most neurotic dog! I realized the dosage she prescribed would keep Timmy drugged at such a level that he would live in a permanent zombie state. That was not an answer I could accept. Disappointed, I handed the prescription back to the doctor: I would not be using it. I paid the two hundred dollar fee and walked out.

I left that day with a heavy heart and a precious dog that looked at me with such love and adoration in his eyes. Timmy trusted me, and I had been so determined to help him, to not let him down, but I felt despair setting in. I didn't know how to help my best friend in the whole world.

LIFE ON A CHAIN

They say sisters share everything. That was certainly the case with two young Lab sisters we named Addison and Madison. They had been chained side by side, sharing filthy, outdoor living quarters and the unfortunate lot of both having litters from their first heat.

Shelley got the call. "There are puppies everywhere! Come get them and take the mommas, too." When Shelley arrived, she found two beautiful sweet momma Labradors, one black and one yellow, and as the caller had said, puppies everywhere. Little fur balls raced between the two chained mommas, running through garbage and filth. There was no shelter available against the bitter cold of winter. Shelley began the process of collecting the mommas and their twelve babies.

It was only after Shelley had the mommas in the car that she heard the woman say, "Oh, we want to keep some of the puppies: two for our friends and one for us." Shelley pleaded with her. She knew what I would say, "Give them the money, whatever they want, but don't leave any behind! Please don't leave any behind!" Often fifty to a hundred dollars goes a long way, but not this time. The woman was adamant about their keeping three. So Shelley gave immunizations to the three pups being left behind, hugged and kissed them, then drove away without them. It was a bittersweet experience. We were thrilled to help these sweet mommas and nine puppies but sad to leave three innocent lives behind to live the life we had just helped the others escape.

Addison and Madison

Once in rescue it was impossible to tell which puppy belonged to which momma, and if the dogs knew they weren't giving any hints. The puppies went from one momma to the next, nursing at both. Good-natured Addison and Madison loved them all. Soon I had nine healthy fluff balls running around my puppy yard, but every time I saw them running and playing, and every time one was placed in the arms of their new family, my heart broke for the three that hadn't made it to rescue. I worried and prayed every day for their health.

(The story continues ...) The Stakeout

A few weeks later both mommas and most of the puppies had found their new homes. They had gone from being chained outside in filthy conditions and the freezing cold to living in homes where they cuddled in bed with their people and spent days hiking and exploring beaches with their families. It seemed to be another happy ending, but I couldn't shake my worry for the three little ones left behind.

Then one day, Kathy, a woman who has her own dog rescue in Yakima, called Shelley. Kathy, usually a dynamic and humorous person, was very serious as she told Shelley that she had reason to believe there were two small puppies locked in a tiny, cold, dark, makeshift enclosure without any windows. They agreed that something needed to be done. These puppies needed to be "borrowed." This is a term rescuers use in the direst circumstances when we need to save dogs: stealing them would not be appropriate, of course, so we "borrow" them.

This rescue attempt would not be easy or quick as the woman who lived in the house was always home. Kathy and her friend staked out the place for several days before they were able to create a plan. Around the same time each day, the owner left for an espresso, but she was never gone long. Time was short though, because in a couple days school would be out for the summer and the neighborhood children would be out and about.

The day of "The Borrowing" came. We were all holding our breath: what if the lady decided that she did not want an espresso that day? We exhaled when, right on schedule, she walked out the front door.

Kathy and her friend were waiting. As soon as the dog owner drove around the corner, they moved in quickly, equipped with tools to break the lock. Cutting the lock took a bit longer than they had hoped, but after a few tense minutes they were able to open the shed door. Kathy grabbed the first puppy, a little white male, and threw him into the arms of her friend who ran back to the van, her heart thudding with fear. The other puppy, a little black female with a white chest and white feet ran to the corner, and Kathy had to run in and grab her fast. There was no time to lovingly assure the little puppy that this was her lucky day. Once in the truck, they sped down the dirt road to where Shelley was waiting for them in her truck. They quickly transferred the frightened puppies to Shelley's truck and drove off in opposite directions.

I was pacing the kitchen floor waiting for Shelley to call me. Finally the phone rang, "Rebecca, we have them. We have the puppies! And guess what? They are Addison's and Madison's babies!" My heart soared. What news! What wonderful, fantastic news!

I'm not sure I ever was so happy to see two puppies. I treasured every moment they were with us and was thrilled when they found their own wonderful families. Caleb now lives in Bellingham, WA near many lakes. Boating and swimming are his favorite pastimes. Sweet Addie is the love of her people's life and such a beauty!

Caleb   Addie

(AND THE STORY STILL CONTINUES ...) BEN

Several months later Shelley got another call. She recognized the voice as the woman who had given up Addison and Madison. "We don't want that puppy anymore. Come and get it."

The last puppy was now safe. This guy, however, was not so little anymore. His cute puppy antics were things of the past: he was now large, strong and untrained.

When Shelley rescued the beautiful dog, he was chained – as he probably had been since the day Shelley rescued his mother, aunt, siblings and cousins. The poor guy had big sores around his neck and no hair where the chain lay, but life as he knew it was about to change! Some may think that being chained for the first eight months of your life would scar your personality and cause irreparable damage to your development. Not for this guy! From the beginning, he was happy and loving of all people and other dogs.

The young pup, now called Benjamin Bear, is a happy, beautiful golden dog that has captured everyone's hearts. Benjamin was

Before Rescue: Ben's Last Day on a Chain

After rescue: Ben's Kingdom

A big smile.

adopted and has loving arms circling his neck instead of a heavy chain. He has a nice soft bed next to a loved one instead of a bed in the snow or having to lie in the hot sun. Benjamin's hard days are past, and he starts each new day with a smile, a butt wiggle and a tail wag.

(And the story never really ends …)

As thrilled as I am – and I am thrilled and proud that Addison and Madison and ALL their puppies were brought into rescue and are living as treasured members of their forever families – there seems to never be an end to the misery. In the same place that Addison and Madison were chained for a year in the cold and filth, and with the same chain that scarred little Ben's neck as he sweltered in the summer heat, another dog is now chained. To some people, dogs seem to be a commodity, easy enough to come by, easy to let go, easy to mistreat. Sometimes there really is only so much a rescuer can do: when I learned about the dog chained where Ben had been, I acquired an igloo-type doghouse to provide some shelter from the winter's bitter cold and summer heat. Shelley took the doghouse out to the site, gave the dog vaccinations, and offered to have it neutered. Now there is nothing to do but wait until the next phone call.

Shoot, It's Just Another Dog.

Desi was driving home one afternoon when she spotted a nursing momma dog wandering alongside the road. Wondering if the dog's litter was safe or needed help, Desi decided she should check it out. The only way to find them was to follow the nursing mother back to her brood. The momma dog was enjoying her morning walk and seemed to be in no hurry to return to her noisy, clamoring bunch. Desi patiently followed the dog along her rather tedious route, and momma dog seemed completely nonplussed by the car following along behind her. Finally, the momma dog turned into a long lane.

What Desi saw made her ill: dogs chained everywhere – all along the lane, in the yard, and behind the barn – and puppies of all ages, darting in and out among the many dogs and abandoned vehicles littering the property. Desi cautiously got out of her car and immediately was drawn to a chained young female who had obviously given birth fairly recently, although she couldn't have been a year old herself. The poor, young mother had puppies of all ages hanging on and nursing from her. What a sweet girl. Her big brown eyes drove darts right into Desi's heart as she leaned into Desi to receive the attention that she craved. Desi fell in love: she wanted nothing more than to help this young dog.

A "lawn-ornament" guard dog sports a heavy chain.

No one answered at the home on the property. Desi contemplated loading the young mother and all the puppies and just driving away with them, but she knew that would prevent her being able to help the many other dogs on the property. With hoarders of this type, the best procedure is to establish a relationship with the family and begin to help as they start to trust you. It is often a long and difficult process, but the only way to help all the dogs in the long run. So it was with a heavy heart that Desi left a note on the door and hugged her new friend good bye, telling her that she would be back very soon to get her.

Sweet momma dog chained in abhorrent living conditions.

Desi was thrilled to receive a call from the lady of the house that evening. The property owner stated that she very definitely wanted help: actually she wanted to get rid of all the dogs, and asked if Desi would come for them. Desi said she needed two days to arrange foster homes and vet visits. The lady seemed quite unhappy that it would take so long, but Desi promised that in two days she would come and get them all.

Desi launched a two-day mission, trying to find foster homes for the numerous dogs and puppies. All her current foster homes were full, so she spent those days in a flurry of calls, contacting everyone she knew and begging people to take just one. She called every vet in the area and tried to find openings for any dogs that were sick, and eventually for spay and neuters.

On the morning of the evacuation, Desi was ready. She had foster homes lined up, people to go with her to gather the dogs, and vets on call with openings. It had been a lot of work to put it together in such a short time, but Desi had done it! She was excited about the opportunity to help so many needy dogs: this was the heart of rescue

Just as she was leaving, Desi received another call from the woman.

"Hi Desi. No need to come by today. I took care of everything last night."

"What … ," Desi's heart stopped. "What is that again?" asked Desi. "How did you take care of everything? What are you talking about?"

"I just took care of everything so you wouldn't have to," the woman said flippantly.

"How did you do that?" asked Desi, who was scared to hear the answer.

"I shot them!"

Stunned, Desi could not believe her ears. "You shot them? You shot who and why? You knew I was coming this morning."

Sweet, surrogate momma dog, befriending the kitty.

"Well, I wasn't sure you would take them all, and I wanted them out of here. So I had someone come last night, shoot them, and haul them away."

Desi was immediately overcome with nausea; she wanted to scream, to weep, to go on her own shooting rampage. The eyes of the young momma dog seared her mind, she had to ask, "Every one … every one … did you shoot every one? Are there any left?" she whispered trying to control the surge of emotions rolling through her.

"Well, there were a couple puppies that escaped under the barn and haven't come out … I guess you can have those if you want to try to get them. I also have a couple for watchdogs, but I'm keeping those."

Desi drove on to the property, which was now empty and quiet. All the dogs that had been barking from their chains were gone. The momma dog whose morning stroll had first led Desi there was gone, as were the puppies that had been scooting in and out among the chaos. Hardest of all for Desi to see was the chain that had held the sweet, young momma dog with big brown eyes: it was laying empty. Desi closed her eyes, but her mind had already sketched an impression of the horrific scene, the dogs' eyes full of fear as they saw death coldly delivered. She asked herself why she hadn't taken them while she could. Why did she think that she needed to wait, to do it properly? Oh, to go back in time! But there is no going back.

Desi crawled under the barn, and with a quiet and reassuring voice lured the frightened puppies from beneath it. She hugged them tightly and sobbed her apologies. On the way to the car, Desi saw two sad dogs chained in the driveway, and her heart broke for them. Summoning all the strength she had to be civil and reasonable she approached the woman and asked if she could make an appointment with her vet, Dr. West, and the rescue would pay to have them neutered. It was not a solution for these dogs, but every step in controlling the prolific breeding of dogs in the area – especially at this house – was a step forward. The lady shrugged her shoulders and said she would have to think about it, as she had heard that Dr. West didn't always treat the dogs kindly. Desi stared at her as she felt every ounce of strength she had put into being civil dissipate. She turned, got into her car and as she drove away she yelled out the window, "What he doesn't do is shoot them!"

One of many innocent
pups whose lives were
lost in the rampage.

A Trip to Nowhere

Puppies, puppies and more puppies; there always seem to be more puppies than space! I have a firm rule: no more than two litters at a time, that number being what I reasonably can manage. With such a firm rule in place it may seem confusing, even to me (maybe especially to me) to read that I often have been supporting three or four, or sometimes more, litters in my rescue. The good news is that the spaying/neutering of pets has started to make a difference in areas such as Seattle, Portland and Vancouver, B.C. As a result, there are fewer unwanted puppies in these urban areas. The bad news is that in rural areas many animals still go unneutered and unwanted litters abound: in fact, most animals in western Washington and Oregon shelters have come from those states' eastern, rural areas. This happens through the efforts of people like Shelley and Desi, who have built relationships with shelter directors in the Portland and Seattle areas to facilitate the placement of puppies and dogs into a network of shelters and rescues where adoption rates are high and loving homes are available. This has helped numerous dogs and puppies from eastern Washington escape the overcrowded, rural shelters, where the majority of dogs do not have a chance of adoption.

Despite the network, there are more puppies than places, and so our rescue was often asked to handle more than two litters. I decided that we needed to expand our network even more. Many of my puppies are adopted to Canadian families. British Columbia (B.C.) seems to be an especially dog-friendly area, one with many dog parks and opportunities for fun canine outings. I decided that I would work with a shelter in British Columbia to see if they would be willing to take Yakima litters that we just couldn't accommodate.

British Columbia rarely has puppies in their humane societies, and we were able to make contact with a shelter director who was willing to take a litter. Still, I was hesitant. I wanted only the best for each puppy, so I decided that I would drive the first litter up myself and meet with the director whom I had been working with over the phone and internet for the past few weeks – just to be sure.

Well, when I say drive up myself, I don't mean literally by myself. As Trulie teases, I have a twenty-minute radius from my house that I will drive by myself. Trulie and Evangelynn suggested we take our own dogs, drop off the puppies and then spend the day at the dog beach at White Rock. So, that morning we loaded our own dogs into the car along with the puppies that had just been transported to us from Yakima, and we headed out for our B.C. adventure!

Although we had been with the puppies only for the morning, I was already becoming attached and was unsure that taking them to the shelter was the right thing to do. However, I had high hopes for this shelter. I was sure they would have a cute puppy room and a puppy yard, and many wonderful applicants to adopt these precious pups.

After several hours of driving we found ourselves pulling into a depressed, industrial setting. The shelter was situated amongst abandoned buildings and warehouses: its urban surroundings were concrete, not the lush green yards that we had hoped to find. We didn't see any yards or play areas.

This is not where I wanted to leave my puppies (and yes, now they had become *my* puppies.) Trulie suggested that we leave the puppies in the car while we look around and talk to the people. *Well, we have driven this far, I might as well do that,* I thought.

Evangelynn stayed in the car while Trulie and I ventured into the building. There were two ladies behind the desk, but they were involved in a conversation and didn't bother to acknowledge us. Trulie shrugged and said, "Well, let's take a look." We walked into a very typical kennel setting: cages on cold cement, housing dogs and perhaps a towel or a lone toy. The dogs seemed bored and sad, and I knew that I wasn't going to leave my puppies there.

"We are not leaving them," I whispered to Trulie.

"Are you sure about this?" Trulie asked.

I was very sure. The decision was made. We now had to figure out how to get out. Now that I had decided, the last thing I wanted to do was to have a conversation with the coordinator who was expecting us. I wanted to avoid talking to anyone. *Maybe there is a back door,* I hoped. There was.

Beyond the back door we found a small sitting area where potential families could meet with the dogs. It was surrounded by an eight foot chain link fence. Perhaps in a slightly irrational moment I suggested we climb it; I just wanted to get out without confrontation. Trulie nodded and said, "We could try climbing it, or we could maybe just walk out the front door, the way we came in. If the women say anything, we will just tell them we were taking a look around; they don't know who we are." That did sound a bit more rational, so I agreed.

Meg, Brynn & Callie
Girls who inspired a little international adventure.

As we walked out, Trulie waved and smiled at the women in the front, but they were so caught up in their conversation they didn't even wave back.

As we approached the car, Evangelynn, who had been playing with the puppies in the back, hopped into the driver's seat and without even waiting for our report, said "Let's go." I barely made it into the car myself before she tore out. Evidently, she also had become attached to the puppies and had no intention of leaving them behind!

On our long trek back home I called Dan.

"Well, hello," he answered. "Was the trip successful?"

"Oh, yes," I answered, "very successful. Could you possibly set up a pen in the garage and make sure it's surrounded with the stand up fans?"

"Uh-huh, I can do that."

I knew he was smiling on the other end.

Girls at play after a long trip.

TOVEE

I loved our puppies, each one of them, but there was one experience still missing for me. I wanted to help deliver a litter of puppies; to be there from the first minute. I had always wanted to witness firsthand that miraculous moment.

Pregnant dogs constantly come into the Yakima rescue, but the logistics of my home and rescue made it impractical to accept one at Lil' Waif. Our dogs were a well-established pack and we were in a subdivision with a small yard; another adult dog was just not feasible. Each time the desire welled up, I recalled all of the reasons that it wouldn't work and told myself to be content in my role of caring for puppies.

So each time Desi or Shelley had a momma dog, I would attempt to live vicariously through them. When the time came near I would call daily to check on the momma dog: had her temperature dropped, had her milk come in, and was she restless or nesting? When they had a momma dog whelping, they were told to call me each time a puppy was born, no matter the time, and share every detail with me.

Desi called one afternoon to tell me about a pregnant, feral dog running loose on the Indian reservation. She was about 20 lbs and needed a foster home, as she looked like she was going to give birth any day. Both Desi and Shelley had nursing moms and other foster dogs; neither of them could take her.

Desi knew I couldn't take an adult dog into my home! I had told her the reasons many times, just as I had told myself. What if my neighbors found out? Running a dog rescue in a neighborhood was already a bit unconventional and risky: I had only been able to get away with it because I had puppies and not adult dogs. I couldn't leave her downstairs in the puppy room, so would she fit in with my dogs upstairs? What if she was protective of her puppies or aggressive? The whole situation made me very nervous. This time, Desi didn't seem to hear me. She told me that I was the only hope for the little momma running alone, pregnant in the woods, ready to give birth.

I could not let her give birth by herself: my conscience wouldn't allow it. Reluctantly, I agreed.

I set up an area that I thought would be comfortable for the momma dog to have her litter. I chose a place that provided her with her own space but was close to the activities of the family, so we could watch her. The day Desi went out to fetch her, I waited anxiously by the phone. The man who had been feeding the momma dog had agreed to hold her in his house until Desi arrived. Desi called me, but not with good news: the guy had left the door open, and the pregnant dog had taken off. Desi had searched, but the area included a large field and woods; it was hopeless.

It had been a long trip for Desi, and we were all discouraged – but I was also almost frantic with worry. I worried that she had run off to have her babies by herself. I worried about her struggling to give birth with no help. I worried about coyotes. I worried that we wouldn't be able to help her and her puppies. I had been hesitant to bring her into my home, but now I was desperate to have her here!

A few days later the man called again, saying that the dog had come back for the food he had been leaving out, and he had caught her. He agreed to meet Desi to turn her over to rescue. I didn't want to get my hopes up, in case she escaped again, and so I was filled with relief and anticipation when Desi phoned to say, "I have her." Within a few minutes, we were in our car, driving to meet my new momma dog, whom we named Tovee.

I soon had on my lap a very scared little girl. Although very pregnant, she was so thin that her ribs were sticking out. She was filthy and had ticks on her body. As I held her on that drive home, I hoped for a smooth adjustment and worried about what I had gotten myself into.

Tovee was a little overwhelmed by our dogs: she immediately found a spot on the couch and did not move from it. We could not even lure her off the couch to go outside for a bathroom break. We carried her out periodically, where she would quickly do her business, then frantically rush back to her spot on the couch, where she felt safe. We brought Tovee food and water because she would not leave the couch to eat or drink. The transition to living in a house with dogs and people was not an easy one for her. Good naturedly, we started calling her "Princess Tovee," as we all bustled around trying to meet her every need.

Tovee

I was sure she was ready to deliver the day we met her; she was so big and uncomfortable. However, days went by with no sign of Tovee going into labor. The birthing pen stood ready, prepared with everything I thought she might possibly need, and I watched and waited attentively, afraid to go to bed at night lest she need me and I miss it. A week passed, and then finally, Tovee started showing signs of labor. She was restless and nervous, constantly moving her blankets around and nesting. It was time!! I was really going to do this; be a part of Tovee's puppies' births. I pulled out all my supplies and laid them on the counter. I had several books (with pages marked, so I could quickly refresh myself with information) along with everything else I thought I might need for the big event. I was ready!! I moved my recliner next to her pen, as I knew it was going to be a long night. Both Dan and Evangelynn were hesitant to go to bed and leave me by myself, but I assured them that I was fine. I was feeling calm and confident, certain that I could handle whatever was to come.

Around midnight Tovee started having contractions. She looked at me with her big brown eyes, full of fear, wanting help, asking for help. All my confidence and bravado drained away in one quick second. *I cannot do this by myself!* I ran and woke up Dan. "I need help with Tovee!" He was immediately concerned until I reassured him: there wasn't anything specifically wrong, it was just that Tovee was having babies.

"I know she is having babies," he said. "I thought you said you could handle it." He looked like he was ready to head back to bed.

"Forget what I said," I retorted. "You are my husband and you are supposed to support me."

I then ran and awoke Evangelynn, who was as thrilled as Dan to be woken up, but also stumbled out of bed to support me.

I sat with Tovee in her pen during the painful contractions, and Dan and Evangelynn stood leaning over us, half asleep. Then I saw it, a small dark form with big, round eyes in a tight sack. It reminded me of a small mouse (which for someone who is petrified of mice, was not comforting). I held up my hands as I started to panic, "I don't know what to do." Maybe I really didn't want this experience. Maybe being part of the birthing process was not what I thought it was going to be. I was rapidly reassessing this whole thing.

Dan suggested that I follow the instructions in the books. "You know, the ones you have been reading all week." He was attempting to be helpful.

Fortunately for us, Tovee knew exactly what to do. Her instinct took over. She cleaned her little guy up nicely, and we helped him begin to nurse while we waited for the next arrival. Tovee had a few more contractions and out came another little guy, this one brown but without white markings around the eyes. He was a robust little puppy and took right to nursing. A third puppy came fast and without much effort, and we now had three little boys. With that, Tovee relaxed. She seemed proud of her brood and was starting to doze. A book I had read said that once the dog seems to relax, you can be pretty sure she has finished delivering. Tovee was a little dog, and three seemed like a perfect number for her. All the puppies were healthy and robust. I was relieved and grateful that all had gone well. Dan and Evangelynn said good night and sauntered back to bed.

I laid back in my chair, ready for all of us to rest now. I was admiring Tovee and her three boys and telling her what a wonderful job she had done when up she jumped with another contraction! Soon a little black girl had been born. She had arrived quick and easy! I woke Dan with the news; we were all excited to have a little girl. On the way back to the living room, I heard Tovee stirring in her pen. I rushed there in time to see her give birth to another black little girl. Puppy number five! Then again, Tovee surprised us with a sixth baby, a baby boy as black as coal. Where had such a small dog put so many babies? I woke Dan with each new birth announcement. He was a good sport; excited about each puppy.

Tovee settled in and I was relieved to know we were done. I wasn't sure how such a small dog was going to nurse six puppies. Whoever had sired this bunch was a large dog, and these were big puppies for such a small mommy. I laid on my side, dozing and watching Tovee sleep as the puppies were nursing. Out of the corner of my eye I saw a puppy slide out. Tovee had not moved; not with a contraction, nor to care for the puppy. She just laid there, too exhausted to move. I jumped up, grabbed the baby and tore off the puppy's sac, and then I held her in front of Tovee so she could lick her baby. Soon, pup number seven was breathing. She was a beautiful multi-colored girl.

I'm not sure who was more proud of her babies, Tovee or me. Every day was special for me: I loved watching them grow, watching their eyes open, watching them learn to scoot across the pen and then eventually walk and play in the pen. I thought each and every one was beautiful. I was concerned about Tovee, though. She was a small girl (even smaller, now that her pregnant belly was gone) and her babies were quite big. They nursed hard on Tovee, yanking and pulling. Tovee, even from the beginning, seemed overwhelmed by her large brood.

Lil' Waif's puppy wing

At three weeks Tovee got mastitis, an infection in the nipples. The vet thought that we could try giving her antibiotics and continue allowing her to nurse, but the mastitis only worsened. One Sunday morning when I awoke, I found that Tovee had dug a hole in her chest from rubbing at it to try to relieve the pain. I had to go to work that day, but Evangelynn rushed Tovee to the emergency vet. Tovee had a high temperature, and the doctor said that she was no longer able to nurse. Well … we had hand fed three-week-old puppies before: we could do it again. What we had not anticipated was the strength of Tovee's instinct to nurse and care for her babies. We moved the babies downstairs, thinking that it would be better if she were without the constant reminder, but Tovee just paced upstairs. Once she even climbed the banister and jumped over and down a flight of stairs to try to reach the puppy room; however, when we put Tovee with her puppies she would do anything to get away from them, as the mastitis caused her so much pain.

What was amazing was to watch Tovee develop some personality and become more confident. She really wasn't much more than a puppy herself, and she had spent her whole life trying to survive. She began to play with our dogs and discovered toys and treats. It was great fun to watch her bloom as her puppies grew big and spunky and became their own little personalities as well. When it was time for them to be adopted into their own homes, they each went to a family that thought their puppy was as special as I did. Tovee, too, found her loving home, where she continues to be "the pampered princess" and no longer has to worry about surviving.

What would have become of Tovee if she had been left in the wild to give birth? There would have been no blankets, no cottage cheese, no pampering, and finally there would have been no medical care for her mastitis. I'm not sure that any of them would have survived.

Much later, Desi and Shelley let it slip that the whole situation had been a set up! They had decided that it was time for me to have the experience I had longed for; so when this little pregnant dog needed help, they agreed they would both refuse to foster her, knowing that I would eventually cave in and take her. I was oblivious to their scheme!

Irresistibly cute!

I am grateful for my experience to witness and be a part of Tovee and her puppies' journey. I am so glad that I said "yes" to Tovee.

A Shadow through the Storm

A dog sat staring at the few cars passing it near the intersection of two lonely mountain roads.

"Mom, black dog … tried to get it to come … scared … my dogs barking … icy road … placed treats, too scared … it's snowing … I don't want to leave it."

That afternoon, Evangelynn had taken her dogs hiking on some old mountain logging roads, and it was her frantic voice on the other end of the phone. The phone reception was poor, and her dogs were barking; communication was almost impossible.

Evangelynn went back the next day, and the next, using food to try luring this lost dog to safety; trying to gain its trust. Every day, the dog sat right at the edge of the woods, watching each car; perhaps waiting for a car he recognized and hoped would return. As soon as a car would stop, however, the dog would slink back into the woods and become a phantom among the trees.

The mountain road is about a thirty-minute drive from the rural community where Trulie teaches, and she soon took on the task of making sure the dog was fed every day. Most days she did not even get a glimpse of the dog, but she knew it was there among the trees, waiting and watching for her to leave so he could have his breakfast. Trulie's rare sightings told us that the dog had a horrible back-leg limp, that huge patches of fur were missing, and that he was so skinny that bones underneath the skin were visible, even from a distance.

One morning Trulie called on her way up to the mountainous intersection, "It snowed last night, I will be able to follow his footprints in the fresh snow… I'm going to catch the dog. I have to, the temperature is falling way below zero tonight. I can't leave him out here anymore." Forty-five minutes later, Trulie called again. This time the determination in her voice had been replaced with despair. "He just stays out of reach. He doesn't run, but I can't get him. I'm late for work, and I'm soaking wet."

We were finally able to locate and borrow a humane animal trap from a local rescue. We were all sure this was the answer, that this would work. Dan, Trulie and I met up on the road and set up the trap close to where the dog sat each day watching the cars. We camouflaged the trap the best we could and placed inside it the most aromatic and tempting treats we could find. The next morning, Trulie made the trek up the mountain, sure that the trap would hold our elusive phantom. The trap stood empty that day. Trulie stopped feeding him, hoping that when the dog became hungry enough it would go for the food in the trap, but days went by without the bait being taken. We had to declare defeat. This dog would rather starve to death than go into the enclosure. And starving to death was exactly what he was doing.

We had to try a different tactic. Meanwhile the dog was cold, wet, and hungry. My friend, Jane, and I drove up with an igloo doghouse, heavy blankets, hay, tarps and plenty of dog food. We walked into the woods and found the very shallow hole he had dug to lay in, under a tree. We set up his new doghouse, stocked it with warm hay and blankets and left plenty of food. It would have to do until we came up with another plan.

One day Trulie called in desperation. "The poor thing could barely even stand to get away from me this morning when I went into the woods to feed it. He's suffering. It's below freezing up here, and the wind is awful. We can't let him die suffering." Trulie thought that the dog's hip issue and health was so bad that the most humane thing would be euthanasia. She couldn't bear letting this dog slowly freeze to death.

We made a plan, one that is risky and not usually advisable, but we were now desperate. We decided that Saturday morning we would put a sedative in the dog's food. A team of volunteers would then go into the woods and search. Our hope was that we would find the guy passed out, cozily curled up in the doghouse. Of course, no such luck. The group of volunteers spread out and scoured the woods. We traipsed through the wooded area that Shadow had called home for the last few weeks. Small trails had been formed, leading down to the creek and around a small perimeter. We went over logs, checked under logs, and made our way around trees, through bushes and thorns. Shadow eluded us.

As minutes turned into hours, the concern grew that Shadow may have become disoriented, wandered away and passed out in the cold. We worried that he might die of exposure or that the sedation itself had been too much for a dog in such poor shape. We all began to feel hopeless. We didn't want to give up, but how many times can you walk the same set of trails, check under the same logs, or go through the same bushes before it becomes an exercise in futility? Shadow had pulled off another disappearing act. Exhausted and cold, the group headed back to their cars, disappointed and worried.

A volunteer shouted, "Wait! He's here! He's here, right next to the car!"

We all came rushing out of the woods to find Shadow standing next to one of the cars, drunk from the sedation and exhausted from trying to elude all the volunteers. We didn't know how the dog was going to react to being handled or approached, so it was decided that one volunteer would throw a blanket over the dog and pick him up, while the rest of us stood nearby, ready to approach if needed. Shadow, too tired and too sedated to resist, was easily picked up and placed in a crate with plenty of blankets.

As I pet Shadow's head, the ordeal seemed surreal to me. All the weeks of trying to gain his trust, all the trips to feed him, the disappointment of the trapping plan, the fear that he wasn't going to make it through a bitter cold night, the long and frustrating exercise this morning, trying to track him, and now here he was. Warm and safe … rescued. "We are going to help you, I promise," I whispered in his ear as I clasped the crate closed.

We took Shadow straight to the vet's office, where our vet was waiting. We were all worried about the condition of Shadow. We knew he was deathly thin, his hip appeared to be injured and most of his fur was gone, but we didn't know what this meant. Were these fatal conditions? Were there other health issues? There were many questions to be answered. Shadow was sweet enough under sedation, but would he be hysterical or aggressive when it wore off?

We waited anxiously as Shadow was bathed, x-rays were taken and a thorough examination conducted. The prognosis was better than we had hoped. The hip looked like an old injury, perhaps the result of having been hit by a car. Everything else was the result of malnutrition and harsh living conditions. With proper care the dog would be fine.

"She is sure a sweet girl," our vet stated. A girl? We were surprised: this whole time Shadow had been a male in our minds. Shadow had obviously had many litters and things had shifted, so from a distance she had appeared to be a male.

Now that we had her up close, and could really look at her, we could see what she had endured. She had a prominently outlined rib cage, jutting hip bones, and an exposed spine, plus considerable hair loss from malnutrition. Her teeth looked as if they had been filed down, worn from gnawing her way out of something, and her stools were full of twigs, small rocks, pine needles and grass. Her big brown eyes, however, seemed to speak right to your soul.

Shadow was handed over to her new foster mom, Jane, and she limped out of the vet's office compliantly on her new leash, settled in the back seat of the car and began her journey of recovery. Shadow acted as if she had always been a house dog, loving all the family members, approaching them for attention and the many treats they gave her as rewards. She began to thrive, her hair growing in thick and shiny, her weight starting to return, and a bouncy and playful personality emerging. She enjoyed all the dogs in the home and even befriended the kitty.

Shadow's life is a happy one. She was adopted by a family who loves and adores her. Shadow has a special bond with "her girl" with whom she sleeps, and she spends her days romping in her family's large back yard and sharing her space on the family couch. We will never know where Shadow, now named Besa, came from, but her present and future are bright.

A Happy Ending: Shadow and her girl

TO EACH PUPPY

Each puppy that comes to us has their own special story. We have saved puppies from pit bull rings, from old boxes alongside the road, and from pregnant mommy dogs that have strayed into our paths. I am overwhelmed with gratitude for each puppy that I have had the opportunity to love, hold and help find a life worth living. Each puppy – those born and those yet to be born – deserves to have the love of their own family, to feel secure and be protected from hunger, loneliness and the unknowns of living as an unwanted dog. That is what Lil' Waif is here to help accomplish.

TIMMY'S JOURNEY

"They're the best trainers! How could you not know about them?" asked the woman who was referring me to a training center that specialized in dogs with behavior problems. It was a good question ... how could I have not heard about them? In my determination to find help for Timmy I had gone through a litany of trainers. Despite my best efforts, it seemed that Timmy grew worse with each trainer and each visit. But, if these were the "best" trainers, well I had nothing to lose. Maybe they were the ones who would finally be able to pinpoint the elusive solution to Timmy's problems.

I met with two women who listened to my story as Timmy paced back and forth in the office, drooling. They patiently explained their procedure for working through fear aggression with dogs. I told them I had been told by other trainers that Timmy might not only be fear aggressive but prey-driven. They didn't seem to think that was an issue, and reassured me.

The plan was that one trainer would stand in the parking lot with a well-behaved Newfoundland mix while the other trainer walked Timmy around him with a loose leash. If Timmy had a reaction, they would pull him in by his leash, reassure him, and then repeat the procedure. The idea was that the trainer would eventually be able to walk Timmy in smaller concentric circles around the dog without a reaction; a desensitizing exercise. I felt uneasy about this plan and objected, saying that Timmy could be very strong. The women, however, seemed confident: they knew what they were doing and had done it many times. I reluctantly agreed. They patted me reassuringly on the shoulder and told me not to worry so much.

The trainer who was going to work with Timmy put a leash on him and he compliantly walked out to the parking lot with her. Once they had walked around a bit and become acquainted with each other they brought out the Newfie. Even from a distance I could see the shadows come into Timmy's eyes, and his mood shift. Timmy lunged. The next thing I knew he was dragging the trainer across the parking lot with her screaming at him to stop. I started yelling at the woman with the Newfie, "Get the dog back inside! Get him in!" She seemed to snap into action just in time, squeezing herself and the dog through the door and slamming it shut just before Timmy lunged at the door in one of his dark fits. I ran to him, and in his typical fashion he snapped out of it just as fast as he had gone into it. He seemed confused and needy, leaning into me.

"This is not fear aggression, and we are sorry he can't be helped." The words cut deep. Maybe it was the first time that my heart heard what my head had known for awhile. There was no help for Timmy. I couldn't help him, and he wasn't safe. I loved him, and because of that, maybe I had to make the hard choices for him. I drove to my vet's office, and quietly told the receptionist that my dog needed to be put down. My vet came out immediately and ushered me back to a small room. I sat in a chair with Timmy's head on my lap and cried so hard I could barely talk. I tried to explain Timmy's issues and how he wasn't safe and that his quality of life was so diminished with his house arrest, severe and constant pain in his leg, and unbearable allergies. My vet comforted me, but she had never seen Timmy behaving worse than a little neurotic. Realizing how upset I was, she convinced me to go home and think about it.

Dan and Evangelynn were shocked and horrified when I told them what I had come close to doing. They both loved Timmy, and each had their own special relationship with him. They were sure that we could continue to work with him, and that we could work it out. I started to feel like perhaps the vet was correct.

A few days later while working down in the puppy room, I heard a scuffle upstairs and ran up to see what was happening. I found Evangelynn looking quite shaken and anxious. She wouldn't talk about what happened, but just said that she was trying to put the dogs out and that Timmy got upset. I found this strange, and was confused. Timmy was never anything but compliant and sweet at home. Timmy, for his part, was laying serenely in the living room. It wasn't until later that Evangelynn was able to confide in me that, at that moment, she had felt like Timmy was going to attack her. This scared me, because he had never been aggressive towards any person, let alone towards Evangelynn, whom he adored.

The next day, I was out in the back yard with the dogs. Our neighbors have a couple of dogs that come out to bark at our dogs when they are out. Our dogs, of course, bark back until we tell them to be quiet or to come inside. Timmy, though, would often escalate to the point of attacking the fence. It was a daily problem, but one that we had never really been able to resolve. This day, Timmy seemed quite a bit more worked up than usual. He wouldn't come in when I called him, so I walked over to grab his collar, like I had done a million times before. This time, Timmy turned on me in his dark way. He flashed his teeth and looked at me with raging eyes, the same fierce eyes I had seen before but had never had directed at me. I realized I was in danger. I ran to the back door and slammed it behind me as Timmy attacked it like a rabid dog. I leaned up against it, my legs weak with the knowledge that although we may have won some battles in Timmy's short three and a half years, at that moment, Timmy and I, together, had lost the war.

A phone call was made to my vet and she agreed to come to the house. This would make it less stressful for Timmy, who had become anxious and neurotic at the vet's office. This time it wasn't an emotional decision. This time Dan and Evangelynn would be there, to be a part of Timmy's death, just as they had been so much a part of his life. Timmy lay sprawled on the couch over my lap, his favorite position. I tried to be brave but bravery failed me. The sobs and tears just kept coming. I was out of control with grief. My precious Timmy, my boy Timmy; he was my best friend, and I was his. Timmy trusted me to his death.

Our veterinarian was patient and kind but firm about placing a muzzle on Timmy before giving him the shot. Timmy was accustomed to muzzles but did question me with a look. I reassured him all was well and the muzzle would be taken off soon. Our vet quickly performed the procedure, and I felt Timmy relax. Shortly thereafter, he died on my lap. We took his body to the vet's office, but I was only able to hold and cuddle Timmy for a short time. The office was closing, and Timmy needed to be placed in the cold room to await his cremation. I mournfully laid Timmy on the hard cold floor and I wrapped my boy in his favorite blanket. No more soft couches or beds with pillows … One more kiss, and the door was closed.

Timmy was my first rescue, and his memory lives on with each puppy that is adopted into his or her forever home. I dedicate this book to Timmy. He was my boy, my star. He taught me so much about love and commitment. Timmy and I rode the highs and lows together, and I truly believe he is waiting for me to cross that Rainbow Bridge so we can once again be reunited.

MEET LIL' WAIF'S CO-FOUNDERS

Rebecca has always loved the idea of protecting the most vulnerable. She is the mother of five daughters, four of whom came to her through adoption. She now rescues puppies, surrounding herself with precious, four-legged children.

Timmy was Rebecca's first puppy since childhood and Lil' Waif's first rescue. Rebecca co-runs Lil' Waif, a rescue that saves the lives of orphan puppies and finds loving families for them to call home. She attributes her love for rescue to knowing that a dog can sometimes bring out the best in all of us. A devoted animal lover, she shares her life with family in Washington State.

As co-founder of Lil' Waif, Evangelynn is passionate about finding ways to help people, especially through the means of matching furry friends with loving families. She has three wonderful canine kiddos; the best little adventurers, who are her constant companions. When not on an alpine trail with her dogs, studying for finals or working on rescue, Evangelynn is happy to share the simple gifts that dogs seem to bring effortlessly; that of love, inspiration and devoted companionship. She also enjoys time with the wonderful friends and family she loves.